BY CHARLES BUKOWSKI
AVAILABLE FROM ECCO

CHARLES BUKOWSKI

THE ROOMINGHOUSE MADRIGALS

EARLY SELECTED POEMS 1946-1966

ecco

An Imprint of HarperCollinsPublishers

THE ROOMINGHOUSE MADRIGALS: EARLY SELECTED POEMS 1946-1966. Copyright ©
1960, 1962, 1963, 1965, 1968, 1988 by Charles Bukowski. All rights reserved. Printed
in the United States of America. No part of this book may be used or reproduced in any
manner whatsoever without written permission except in the case of brief quotations
embodied in critical articles and reviews. For information, address HarperCollins
Publishers, 195 Broadway, New York, NY 10007.

HarperCollins books may be purchased for educational, business, or sales promotion-
al use. For information, please e-mail the Special Markets Department at
SPsales@harpercollins.com.

Grateful acknowledgment is given to the editors of the scores of literary magazines and
chapbooks where many of these poems originally appeared. Thanks also to Chris Brun,
Special Collections Librarian at the University of California, Santa Barbara for his
cooperation. And finally, thanks to Michael J. Sherick for his assistance in locating
these texts.

First Ecco edition published in 2002
Previously published by Black Sparrow Press

The Library of Congress has catalogued a previous edition as follows:
Bukowski, Charles. 1920-1994.
The roominghouse madrigals.

I. Title.
PS3552.U4A6   1988   811'.54   88-10426
ISBN 0-87685-733-0
ISBN 0-87685-732-2 (pbk.)

HB 06.09.2023

Foreword

A question put to me quite often is, "Why do your out-of-print books cost so much?" Well, they cost so much because that's what booksellers can get for them from collectors.

"I want to read your early poems but . . ."

I don't even have some of my early books. Most of them were stolen by people I drank with. When I'd go to the bathroom, they did *their* shit. It only reinforced my general opinion of humanity. And caused me to drink with fewer people.

At first, I made efforts to replace these books, and did, but when they were stolen all over again I stopped the replacement process and more and more drank alone.

Anyhow, what follows are what we consider to be the best of the early poems. Some are taken from the first few books; others were not in books but have been taken from obscure magazines of long ago.

The early poems are more lyrical than where I am at now. I like these poems but I disagree with some who claim, "Bukowski's early work was much better." Some have made these claims in critical reviews, others in parlors of gossip.

Now the reader can make his own judgment, first hand.

In my present poetry, I go at matters more directly, land on them and then get out. I don't believe that my early methods and my late methods are either inferior or superior to one another. They are different, that's all.

Yet, re-reading these, there remains a certain fondness for that time. Coming in from the factory or warehouse, tired enough, there seemed little use for the night except to eat, sleep and then return to the menial job. But there was the typewriter waiting for me in those many old rooms with torn shades and worn rugs, the tub and toilet down the hall, and the feeling in the air of all the losers who had preceded me. Sometimes the typewriter was there when the job wasn't and the food wasn't and the rent wasn't. Sometimes the typer was in hock. Sometimes there was only the park bench. But at the best of times there was the small room and the machine and the bottle. The sound of the keys, on and on, and shouts: "HEY! KNOCK

IT OFF, FOR CHRIST'S SAKE! WE'RE WORKING PEOPLE HERE AND WE'VE GOT TO GET UP IN THE MORNING!" With broomsticks knocking on the floor, pounding coming from the ceiling, I would work in a last few lines. . . .

I was not Hamsun eating his own flesh in order to continue writing but I had a fair amount of travail. The poems were sent out as written on first impulse, no line or word changes. I never revised or retyped. To eliminate an error, I would simply go over it thus: #########, and go on with the line. One magazine editor printed a group of my poems with all the ########s intact.

At any rate, here are many of the poems from that wondrous and crazy time, from those distant hours. The room steamed with smoke, dizzied with fumes, we gambled. I hope they work for you. And if they don't, well, #### ## ###.

Charles Bukowski
San Pedro, 10-31-87

Table of Contents

THE ROOMINGHOUSE MADRIGALS:
EARLY SELECTED POEMS 1946–1966

22,000 Dollars in 3 Months

night has come like something crawling
up the bannister, sticking out its tongue
of fire, and I remember the
missionaries up to their knees in muck
retreating across the beautiful blue river
and the machine gun slugs flicking spots of
fountain and Jones drunk on the shore
saying shit shit these Indians
where'd they get the fire power?
and I went in to see Maria
and she said, do you think they'll attack,
do you think they'll come across the river?
afraid to die? I asked her, and she said
who isn't?
and I went to the medicine cabinet
and poured a tall glassful, and I said
we've made 22,000 dollars in 3 months building roads
for Jones and you have to die a little
to make it that fast . . . Do you think the communists
started this? she asked, do you think it's the communists?
and I said, will you stop being a neurotic bitch.
these small countries rise because they are getting
their pockets filled from *both* sides . . . and she
looked at me with that beautiful schoolgirl idiocy
and she walked out, it was getting dark but I let her go,
you've got to know when to let a woman go if you want to
    keep her,
and if you don't want to keep her you let her go anyhow,
so it's always a process of letting go, one way or the other,
so I sat there and put the drink down and made another
and I thought, whoever thought an engineering course at Old Miss
would bring you where the lamps swing slowly
in the green of some far night?
and Jones came in with his arm around her blue waist
and she had been drinking too, and I walked up and said,

man and wife? and that made her angry for if a woman can't
get you by the nuts and squeeze, she's done,
and I poured another tall one, and
I said, you 2 may not realize it
but we're not going to get out of here alive.

we drank the rest of the night.
you could hear, if you were real still,
the water coming down between the god trees,
and the roads we had built
you could hear animals crossing them
and the Indians, savage fools with some savage cross to bear.
and finally there was the last look in the mirror
as the drunken lovers hugged
and I walked out and lifted a piece of straw
from the roof of the hut
then snapped the lighter, and I
watched the flames crawl, like hungry mice
up the thin brown stalks, it was slow but it was
real, and then not real, something like an opera,
and then I walked down toward the machine gun sounds,
the same river, and the moon looked across at me
and in the path I saw a small snake, just a small one,
looked like a rattler, but it couldn't be a rattler,
and it was scared seeing me, and I grabbed it behind the neck
before it could coil and I held it then
its little body curled around my wrist
like a finger of love and all the trees looked with eyes
and I put my mouth to its mouth
and love was lightning and remembrance,
dead communists, dead fascists, dead democrats, dead gods and
back in what was left of the hut Jones
had his dead black arm around her dead blue waist.

On Seeing an Old Civil War Painting
with My Love

I

the cannoneer is dead,
and all the troops;

the conceited drummer boy
dumber than the tombs
lies in a net of red;

and under leaves, bugs twitch antennae
deciding which way to move
under the cool umbrella of decay;

the wind rills down like thin water
and searches under clothing,
sifting and sorry;

. . . clothing anchored with heavy bones
in noonday sleep
like men gone down on ladders, resting;

yet an hour ago
tree-shadow and man-shadow
showed their outline against the sun—

yet now, not a man amongst them
can single out the reason
that moved them down toward nothing;

and I think mostly of some woman far off
arranging important jars on some second shelf
and humming a dry, sun-lit tune.

outside, the quick storm turns the night slowly
backwards
and sends it shifting to old shores,
and everywhere are bones . . . rib bones and light,
and grass, grass leaning left;
and we hump our backs against the wet like living things,
and this one with me now
holds my yearning like a packet
slips it into her purse with her powders and potions
pulls up a sheer stocking, chatters, touches her hair:
it's raining, oh damn it all, it's raining!
and on the battlefield the rocks are wet and cool,
the fine grains of rock glint moon-fire,
and she curses under a small green hat
like a crown
and walks like a gawky marionette
into the strings of rain.

What to Do with Contributor's Copies?

(Dear Sir: Although we realize it is
insufficient payment for your poems,
you will receive 4 contributor's copies,
which we will mail directly to you or to
anyone you wish. —Note from the Editor.)

well, ya better mail one to M.S. or she'll prob.
put her pisser in the oven, she thinks she is hot
stuff, and mabe she is, I sure as hell wd't
know
then there is C.W. who does not answer his mail
but is very busy teaching young boys how to write
and I know he is going places, and since he is,
ya better mail 'm one . . .
                                    then there's my old aunt in
Palm Springs   nothing but money   and I have
everything but money . . . talent, a good singing voice,
a left hook deep to the gut . . . send her a copy,
she hung up on me, last time I phoned her drunk,
giving evidence of need, she hung up
on me . . .
                    then there's this girl in Sacramento who
writes me these little letters . . . very depressed
bitch, mixed and beaten like some waffle, making
gentle intellectual overtures which I ignore,
but send her a magazine
                            in lieu of a hot poker.

that makes 4?
                    I hope to send you some more poems
                    soon because I figure that
                    people who print my poems are a little
                    mad, but that's all right. I am also
                    that way. anyhow—

I hope
     meanwhile
          you do not fold up
before
    I
      do.
              c.b.

Brave Bull

I did not know
                  that the Mexicans
                                did this:
                                        the bull
had been brave
              and now
                      they dragged him
                                      dead
around the ring
                by his
                      tail,
                          a brave bull
                                      dead,
but not just another bull,
                          this was a special
                                            bull,
and to me
          a special
                    lesson . . .
                                and although Brahms
stole his *First* from Beethoven's
                                  9th.
                                  and although
the bull
        was dead
                his head and his horns and
his insides dead,
                  he had been better than
                                          Brahms,
                                                  as good as
                                                  Beethoven,

and

as we walked out
                    the sound and meaning
                                        of him
kept crawling up my arms
and although people bumped me and
stepped on my toes
the bull burned within me
                    my candle of
                                        jesus,
dragged by his tail
                    he had nothing to do
                                        having done it all,
and through the long tunnels and minatory glances,
the elbows and feet and eyes, I prayed for California,
and the dead bull
              in man
                    and in me,
              and I clasped my hands
                                        deep within my
pockets, seized darkness,
                    and moved on.

It's Not Who Lived Here

but who died here;
and it's not when
but how;
it's not
the known great
but the great who died unknown;
it's not
the history
of countries
but the lives of men.

fables are dreams,
not lies,
and
truth changes
as
men change,
and when truth becomes stable
men
will
become dead
and
the insect
and the fire and
the flood
will become
truth.

O, We Are the Outcasts

ah, christ, what a CREW:
more
poetry, always more
P O E T R Y .

if it doesn't come, coax it out with a
laxative. get your name in LIGHTS,
get it up there in
8½ x 11 mimeo.

keep it coming like a miracle.

ah christ, writers are the most sickening
of all the louts!
yellow-toothed, slump-shouldered,
gutless, flea-bitten and
obvious . . . in tinker-toy rooms
with their flabby hearts
they tell us
what's wrong with the world—
as if we didn't know that a cop's club
can crack the head
and that war is a dirtier game than
marriage . . .
or down in a basement bar
hiding from a wife who doesn't appreciate him
and children he doesn't
want
he tells us that his heart is drowning in
vomit. hell, all our hearts are drowning in vomit,
in pork salt, in bad verse, in soggy
love.
but he thinks he's alone and
he thinks he's special and he thinks he's Rimbaud

and he thinks he's
Pound.

and death! how about death? did you know
that we all have to die? even Keats died, even
Milton!
and D. Thomas—THEY KILLED HIM, of course.
Thomas didn't *want* all those free drinks
all that free pussy—
they . . . FORCED IT ON HIM
when they should have left him alone so he could
write write WRITE!

poets.

and there's another
type. I've met them at their country
places (don't ask me what I was doing there because
I don't know).

they were born with money and
they don't have to dirty their hands in
slaughterhouses or washing
dishes in grease joints or
driving cabs or pimping or selling pot.

this gives them time to understand
Life.

they walk in with their cocktail glass
held about heart high
and when they drink they just
sip.

you are drinking green beer which you
brought with you
because you have found out through the years
that rich bastards are *tight*—

they use 5 cent stamps instead of airmail
they promise to have all sorts of goodies ready
upon your arrival
from gallons of whiskey to
50 cent cigars. but it's never
there.
and they HIDE their women from you—
their wives, x-wives, daughters, maids, so forth,
because they've read your poems and
figure all you want to do is fuck everybody and
everything. which once might have been
true but is no longer *quite*
true.

and—
he WRITES TOO.
POETRY, of
course. *everybody*
writes
poetry.

he has plenty of time and a
postoffice box in town
and he drives there 3 or 4 times a day
looking and hoping for accepted
poems.

he thinks that poverty is a weakness of the
soul.

he thinks your mind is ill because you are
drunk all the time and have to work in a
factory 10 or 12 hours a
night.

he brings his wife in, a beauty, stolen from a
poorer rich
man.

he lets you gaze for 30 seconds
then hustles her
out. she has been crying for some
reason.

you've got 3 or 4 days to linger in the
guesthouse he says,
"come on over to dinner
sometime."
but he doesn't say when or
where. and then you find that you are not even
IN HIS HOUSE.

you are in
ONE of his houses but
his house is somewhere
else—
you don't know
where.

he even has x-wives in some of his
houses.

his main concern is to keep his x-wives away from
you. he doesn't want to give up a
damn thing. and you can't blame him:
his x-wives are all young, stolen, kept,
talented, well-dressed, schooled, with
varying French-German accents.

and!: they
WRITE POETRY TOO. or
PAINT. or
fuck.

but his big problem is to get down to that mail
box in town to get back his
rejected poems

and to keep his eye on all the other mail boxes
in all his other
houses.

meanwhile, the starving Indians
sell beads and baskets in the streets of the small desert
town.

the Indians are not allowed in his houses
not so much because they are a fuck-threat
but because they are
dirty and
ignorant. dirty? I look down at my shirt
with the beerstain on the front.
ignorant? I light a 6 cent cigar and
forget about
it.

he or they or somebody was supposed to meet me at
the
train station.

of course, they weren't
there. "We'll be there to meet the great
Poet!"

well, I looked around and didn't see any
great poet. besides it was 7 a.m. and
40 degrees. those things
happen. the trouble was there were no
bars open. nothing open. not even a
jail.

he's a poet.
he's also a doctor, a head-shrinker.
no blood involved that
way. he won't tell me whether I am crazy or
not—I don't have the
money.

he walks out with his cocktail glass
disappears for 2 hours, 3 hours,
then suddenly comes walking back in
unannounced
with the same cocktail glass
to make sure I haven't gotten hold of
something more precious than
Life itself.

my cheap green beer is killing
me. he shows heart (hurrah) and
gives me a little pill that stops my
gagging.
but nothing decent to
drink.

he'd bought a small 6 pack
for my arrival but that was gone in an
hour and 15
minutes.

"I'll buy you barrels of beer," he had
said.

I used his phone (one of his phones)
to get deliveries of beer and
cheap whiskey. the town was ten miles away,
downhill. I peeled my poor dollars from my poor
roll. and the boy needed a tip, of
course.

the way it was shaping up I could see that I was
hardly Dylan Thomas yet, not even
Robert Creeley. certainly Creeley wouldn't have
had beerstains on his
shirt.

anyhow, when I finally got hold of one of his
x-wives I was too drunk to
make it.

scared too. sure, I imagined him peering
through the window—
he didn't want to give up a damn thing—
and
leveling the luger while I was
working
while "The March to the Gallows" was playing over
the Muzak
and shooting me in the ass first and
my poor brain
later.

"an intruder," I could hear him telling them,
"ravishing one of my helpless x-wives."

I see him published in some of the magazines
now. not very good stuff.

a poem about me
too: the Polack.

the Polack whines too much. the Polack whines about his
country, other countries, all countries, the Polack
works overtime in a factory like a fool, among other
fools with "pre-drained spirits."
the Polack drinks seas of green beer
full of acid. the Polack has an ulcerated
hemorrhoid. the Polack picks on fags
"fragile fags." the Polack hates his
wife, hates his daughter. his daughter will become
an alcoholic, a prostitute. the Polack has an
"obese burned out wife." the Polack has a
spastic gut. the Polack has a
"rectal brain."

thank you, Doctor (and poet). any charge for
this? I know I still owe you for the
pill.

Your poem is not too good
but at least I got your starch up.
most of your stuff is about as lively as a
wet and deflated
beachball. but it is your round, you've won a round.
going to invite me out this
Summer? I might scrape up
trainfare. got an Indian friend who'd like to meet
you and yours. he swears he's got the biggest
pecker in the state of California.

and guess what?
he writes
POETRY
too!

Poem for My 43rd Birthday

To end up alone
in a tomb of a room
without cigarettes
or wine—
just a lightbulb
and a potbelly,
grayhaired,
and glad to have
the room.

. . . in the morning
they're out there
making money:
judges, carpenters,
plumbers, doctors,
newsboys, policemen,
barbers, carwashers,
dentists, florists,
waitresses, cooks,
cabdrivers . . .

and you turn over
to your left side
to get the sun
on your back
and out
of your eyes.

The Genius of the Crowd

There is enough treachery, hatred,
                              violence,
Absurdity in the average human
                         being
To supply any given army on any given
  day.
AND The Best At Murder Are Those
  Who Preach Against It.
AND The Best At Hate Are Those
  Who Preach LOVE
AND THE BEST AT WAR
—FINALLY—ARE THOSE WHO
PREACH
                              PEACE

Those Who Preach GOD
  NEED God
Those Who Preach PEACE
  Do Not Have Peace.
THOSE WHO PREACH LOVE
  DO NOT HAVE LOVE
BEWARE THE PREACHERS
Beware The Knowers.

          Beware
          Those Who
          Are ALWAYS
          READING
          BOOKS

Beware Those Who Either Detest
  Poverty Or Are Proud Of It

BEWARE Those Quick To Praise
For They Need PRAISE In Return

31

BEWARE Those Quick To Censure:
They Are Afraid Of What They Do
Not Know

Beware Those Who Seek Constant
Crowds; They Are Nothing
Alone

>Beware
>The Average Man
>The Average Woman
>BEWARE Their Love

Their Love Is Average, Seeks
Average
But There Is Genius In Their Hatred
There Is Enough Genius In Their
Hatred To Kill You, To Kill
Anybody.

Not Wanting Solitude
Not Understanding Solitude
They Will Attempt To Destroy
Anything
That Differs
From Their Own

>Not Being Able
>To Create Art
>They Will Not
>Understand Art

They Will Consider Their Failure
As Creators
Only As A Failure
Of The World

Not Being Able To Love Fully
They Will BELIEVE Your Love
Incomplete
AND THEN THEY WILL HATE
YOU

And Their Hatred Will Be Perfect
Like A Shining Diamond
Like A Knife
Like A Mountain
LIKE A TIGER
LIKE Hemlock

     Their Finest
     ART

4:30 A.M.

the fields rattle
with red birds;
it is 4:30 in
the morning,
it is always
4:30 in the morning,
and I listen for
my friends:
the garbagemen
and the thieves,
and cats dreaming
red birds
and red birds dreaming
worms,
and worms dreaming
along the bones of
my love,
and I cannot sleep,
and soon morning will come,
the workers will rise,
and they will look for me
at the docks,
and they will say,
"he is drunk again,"
but I will be asleep,
finally,
among the bottles and
sunlight,
all darkness gone,
my arms spread like
a cross,
the red birds
flying,
flying,
roses opening in the smoke,

and
like something stabbed and
healing,
like
40 pages through a bad novel,
a smile upon
my idiot's face.

The Simplicity of Everything
in Viet Nam

man shot through back while
holding robes of a young priest
who looks like a woman,
and here we hang:
moon-bright
neatly gloved,
motorcycles everywhere, bees asleep,
nozzles rusted,
climate awry,
and we shake our bones,
blind skin there,
and the soldier falls dead,
another dead soldier,
the black robe of a young priest
who looks like a woman
is now beautifully red,
and the tanks
come on through.

The Night They Took Whitey

bird-dream and peeling wallpaper
symptoms of grey sleep
and at 4 a.m. Whitey came out of his room
(the solace of the poor is in numbers
like Summer poppies)
and he began to scream *help me! help me! help me!*
(an old man with hair as white as any ivory tusk)
and he was vomiting blood
help me help me help me
and I helped him lie down in the hall
and I beat on the landlady's door
(she is as French as the best wine but as tough as
an American steak) and
I hollered her name, *Marcella! Marcella!*
(the milkman would soon be coming with his
pure white bottles like chilled lilies)
Marcella! Marcella! help me help me help me,
and she screamed back through the door:
you polack bastard, are you drunk again? then
Promethean the eye at the door
and she
sized up the red river in her rectangular brain
(oh, I am nothing but a drunken polack
a bad pinch-hitter a writer of letters to the newspapers)
and she spoke into the phone like a lady ordering bread and
    eggs,
and I held to the wall
dreaming bad poems and my own death
and the men came . . . one with a cigar, the other needing a
    shave,
and they made him stand up and walk down the steps
his ivory head on fire (Whitey, my drinking pal—
all the songs, Sing Gypsy, Laugh Gypsy, talk about
the war, the fights, the good whores,
skid-row hotels floating in wine,

floating in crazy talk,
cheap cigars and anger)
and the siren took him away, except the red part
and I began to vomit and the French wolverine screamed
you'll have to clean it up, all of it, you and Whitey!
and the steamers sailed and rich men on yachts
kissed girls young enough to be their daughters,
and the milkman came by and stared
and the neon lights blinked selling something
tires or oil or underwear
and she slammed her door and I was alone
ashamed
it was the war, the war forever, the war was never over,
and I cried against the peeling walls,
the weakness of our bones, our sotted half-brains,
and morning began to creep into the hall—
toilets flushed, there was bacon, there was coffee,
there were hangovers, and I too
went in and closed my door and sat down and waited for the
   sun.

The Japanese Wife

O lord, he said, Japanese women,
real women, they have not forgotten,
bowing and smiling
closing the wounds men have made;
but American women will kill you like they
tear a lampshade,
American women care less than a dime,
they've gotten derailed,
they're too nervous to make good:
always scowling, belly-aching,
disillusioned, overwrought;
but oh lord, say, the Japanese women:
there was this one,
I came home and the door was locked
and when I broke in she broke out the bread knife
and chased me under the bed
and her sister came
and they kept me under that bed for two days,
and when I came out, at last,
she didn't mention attorneys,
just said, you will never wrong me again,
and I didn't; but she died on me,
and dying, said, you can wrong me now,
and I did,
but you know, I felt worse then
than when she was living;
there was no voice, no knife,
nothing but little Japanese prints on the wall,
all those tiny people sitting by red rivers
with flying green birds,
and I took them down and put them face down
in a drawer with my shirts,
and it was the first time I realized
that she was dead, even though I buried her;
and some day I'll take them all out again,

all the tan-faced little people
sitting happily by their bridges and huts
and mountains—
but not right now,
not just yet.

Sundays Kill More Men Than Bombs

due to weekend conditions, and although there's
too much smog, everything's jammed
and it's worse than masts down in a storm
you can't go anywhere
and if you do, they are all staring through glass windows
or waiting for dinner, and no matter how bad it is
(not the glass, the dinner)
they'll spend more time talking about it
than eating it,
and that's why my wife got rid of me:
I was a boor and didn't know when to smile
or rather (worse) I did,
but didn't, and one afternoon
with people diving into pools
and playing cards
and watching carefully shaven T.V. comedians
in starched white shirts and fine neckties
kidding about what the world had done to them,
I pretended a headache
and they gave me the young lady's bedroom
(she was about 17)
and hell, I crawled beneath her sheets
and pretended to sleep
but everybody knew I was a cornered fake,
but I tried all sorts of tricks—
I tried to think of Wilde behind bars,
but Wilde was dead;
I tried to think of Hem shooting a lion
or walking down Paris streets
medallioned with his wild buddies,
the whores swooning to their beautiful knees,
but all I did was twist within her young sheets,
and from the headboard, shaking in my nervous storm,
several trinkets fell upon me—
elephants, glass dogs with seductive stares,

41

a young boy and girl carrying a pail of water,
but nothing by Bach or conducted by Ormandy,
and I finally gave it up, went into the john
and tried to piss (I knew I would be constipated
for a week), and then I walked out,
and my wife, a reader of Plato and e.e. cummings
ran up and said, "ooooh, you should have *seen*
BooBoo at the pool! He turned backflips and sideflips
and it was the funniest thing you've
EVER seen!''

I think it was not much later that the man came
to our third floor apartment
about seven in the morning
and handed me a summons for divorce,
and I went back to bed with her and said,
don't worry, it's all right, and
she began to cry cry cry,
I'm sorry, I'm sorry, I'm sorry,
and I said, please stop,
remember your heart.

but that morning when she left
about 8 o'clock she looked
the same as ever, maybe even better.
I didn't even bother to shave;
I called in sick and went down
to the corner bar.

The Loser

and the next I remembered I'm on a table,
everybody's gone: the head of bravery
under light, scowling, flailing me down . . .
and then some toad stood there, smoking a cigar:
"Kid you're no fighter," he told me,
and I got up and knocked him over a chair;
it was like a scene in a movie, and
he stayed there on his big rump and said
over and over: "Jesus, Jesus, whatsamatta wit
you?" and I got up and dressed,
the tape still on my hands, and when I got home
I tore the tape off my hands and
wrote my first poem,
and I've been fighting
ever since.

On a Night You Don't Sleep

at the sea at the beach in the dark there was somebody
sitting in a car along the shore and playing this drum
as if in Africa and the cops rode by on the sidewalk
and I went down to the disappointing sea
and saw two blue lights in the water and a boat
and a man walked by in a white shirt and squatted by the
shore and got up and walked along the shore
and then another man came and followed him:
they both walked along the shore by the water
one 12 feet behind the other and I watched them until
they disappeared and then I got up and walked through
the sand to the cement and through a bar door I saw a
negro singing with a light on his face
he wailed a strange song and the sound of the song twisted
in the air and everything was empty and dry and easy
and I got into my car and drove back to the hot city
but I knew I would always remember the time
and the catch of it—the way the night hung undisturbed
with people walking on it like some quiet rug
and a small boat rocking bravely by bulldogging water
and the colored pier lights like a broken mind sick in the sea.

the legs are gone and the hopes—the lava of outpouring,
and I haven't shaved in sixteen days
but the mailman still makes his rounds and
water still comes out of the faucet and I have a photo of
myself with glazed and milky eyes full of simple music
in golden trunks and 12 oz. gloves when I made the semi-finals
only to be taken out by a German brute who should have been
locked in a cage for the insane and allowed to drink blood.
Now I am insane and stare at the wallpaper as one would stare
at a Cézanne or an early Picasso (he has lost it), and I sent out
the girls for beer, the old girls who barely bother to wipe
their asses and say, well, I guess I won't comb my hair today:
it might bring me luck! well, anyway, they wash the dishes and
chop the wood, and the landlady keeps saying let me in, I can't
get in, you've got the lock on, and what's all that singing and
cussing in there? but she only wants a piece of ass, she pretends
she wants the rent
                    but she's not gonna get either one of 'em.
meanwhile the skulls of the dead are full of beetles and
old football scores like S.C. 16, N.D. 14 on a John
Baker field goal.

I can see the fleet from my window, the sails and the guns,
    always
the guns poking their eyes in the sky looking for trouble like
    young
L.A. cops who haven't yet shaved and the young sailors out
there sex-hungry, trying to act tough, trying to act like men
but really closer to their mother's nipples than to a true evalu-
    ation of existence. I say, god damn it, that
the legs are gone and the outpourings too. inside my brain
rats snip and snipe and
                    pour oil
to burn and fire out early dreams.
darling, says one of the girls, you've got to snap out of it,

we're running out of MONEY. how do you want
your toast?
                    light or dark?

a woman's a woman, I say, and I put my binoculars between
    her
kneecaps and I can see where
empires have fallen.

I wish I had a brush, some paint, some paint and a brush, I say.

why? asks one of the
whores

BECAUSE RATS DON'T LIKE OIL! I scream.

(I can't do it. I don't belong here. I listen to radio programs
and people's voices and I marvel that they can get excited
and interested over nothing) and I flick out the lights, I
crash out the lights, and I pull the shades down, I
tear the shades down as I light my last cigar
then dream jump from the Empire State Building
into the thickheaded bullbrained mob with the hard-on attitude;
already forgotten the dead of Normandy, Lincoln's stringy
    beard,
all the bulls that have died to flashing red capes,
all the love that has died in women and men
while fools have been elevated to the trumpet's succulent sneer
and I have fought (red-handed and drunk
in slop-pitted alleys)
the bartenders of this rotten land.

and I laugh, I can still laugh, who can't laugh when the whole
    thing
is so ridiculous
                    that only the insane, the clowns, the half-wits,
the cheaters, the whores, the horseplayers, the bankrobbers, the
poets . . . are interesting?

46

in the dark I hear hands reaching for the last of my money
like mice nibbling at paper, automatic, while I slumber,
a false drunken God asleep at the wheel . . .
a quarter rolls across the floor, and I remember all the faces and
the football heroes, and everything has meaning, and an editor
writes me, you are good
                    but
                        you are too emotional
the way to whip life is to quietly frame the agony,
study it and put it to sleep in the abstract.

is there anything less abstract
                        than dying everyday and
on the last day?

the door closes and the last of the great whores are gone
and they are all great, somehow no matter how they have
killed me, they are great, and I smoke quietly
thinking of Mexico, of the decaying horses and dead bulls,
of Havana and Spain and Normandy, of the jabbering insane,
of the Kamikaze
winning whether they lived or died,
of my dead friends, of no more friends
ever; and the voice of my Mexican buddy saying, you won't die
you won't die in this war, you're too smart, you'll take care
of yourself.

I keep thinking of the bulls. the rotting bulls, dying everyday.
the whores are gone. the shells have stopped for a minute.

fuck everybody.

All I Know

All I know is this: the ravens kiss my mouth,
the veins are tangled here,
the sea is made of blood.

All I know is this: the hands reaching out,
my eyes are closed, my ears are closed,
the sky rejects my scream.

All I know is this: my nostrils drip with dreams
the hounds lap us up, the fools laugh out,
the clock ticks out the dead.

All I know is this: my feet are sorrow here,
my words are less than lilies, my words are clotted now:
the ravens kiss my mouth.

On Going Back to the Street
after Viewing an Art Show

they talk down through
the centuries to us,
and this we need more and more,
the statues and paintings
in midnight age
as we go along
holding dead hands.

and we would say
rather than delude the unknowing:
a damn good show,
but hardly enough for a horse to eat,
and out on the sunshine street where
eyes are dabbled in metazoan faces
I decide again
that in these centuries
they have done very well
considering the nature of their
brothers:
it's more than good
that some of them,
(closer really to field-mouse than
falcon)
have been bold enough to try.

Anthony

and the hedges wet in the rain, flaking in a sheet of wind,
and for a moment everything working: rusty bells, April
birds, unblushing brides, anything you can name that has not
died, so exactly, and even the wind like a lover's hand,
a somehow important wind, something too like sleep or slain
 enemies,
and the feet move through paths not restricted by the
 bull-goaded mind,
and see—all and everywhere—hedges in the rain
like great cathedrals now, new Caesars, cats walking,
new gods without plug or wire, love without wasps,
new Christians, bulls, Romes, new new leaves, new rain
now splashing through the fire; and I close the door, old room,
I fall upon the couch, I sweat
and I cough I cough small words
lions bearing down through coffee cups and puddles, I
sigh, Cleopatra. Not for either of us, but for the rest.

Layover

Making love in the sun, in the morning sun
in a hotel room
above the alley
where poor men poke for bottles;
making love in the sun
making love by a carpet redder than our blood,
making love while the boys sell headlines
and Cadillacs,
making love by a photograph of Paris
and an open pack of Chesterfields,
making love while other men—poor fools—
work.

That moment—to this . . .
may be years in the way they measure,
but it's only one sentence back in my mind—
there are so many days
when living stops and pulls up and sits
and waits like a train on the rails.
I pass the hotel at 8
and at 5; there are cats in the alleys
and bottles and bums,
and I look up at the window and think,
I no longer know where you are,
and I walk on and wonder where
the living goes
when it stops.

The Dogs of Egypt

the dirty dogs of Egypt stride down my bones
the cat goes home in the morning
and I think of agony when there's little else to
do, and there's usually little else to do
except think the agony might kill us—
but, perhaps, what really saves us from it
is our being able to luxuriate in it—
like an old lady putting on a red hat.

yet my walls are stained where broken glass has
pissed its liquor.

I see agony in a box of kitchen soap
and the walls want their flatness to be my
flatness, o the dirty dogs of Egypt,
I see flatirons hanging from hooks
the eagle is a canary in the breakfastnook
eating dry seed and cramped by the dream.

I want so much that is not here and do not know
where to go.

Old Man, Dead in a Room

this thing upon me is not death
but it's as real
and as landlords full of maggots
pound for rent
I eat walnuts in the sheath
of my privacy
and listen for more important
drummers;
it's as real, it's as real
as the broken-boned sparrow
cat-mouthed, uttering
more than mere
miserable argument;
between my toes I stare
at clouds, at seas of gaunt
sepulcher . . .
and scratch my back
and form a vowel
as all my lovely women
(wives and lovers)
break like engines
into steam of sorrow
to be blown into eclipse;
bone is bone
but this thing upon me
as I tear the window shades
and walk caged rugs,
this thing upon me
like a flower and a feast,
believe me
is not death and is not
glory
and like Quixote's windmills
makes a foe
turned by the heavens

against one man;
. . . this thing upon me,
great god,
this thing upon me
crawling like a snake,
terrifying my love of commonness,
some call Art
some call Poetry;
it's not death
but dying will solve its power
and as my grey hands
drop a last desperate pen
in some cheap room
they will find me there
and never know
my name
my meaning
nor the treasure
of my escape.

Love Is a Piece of Paper Torn to Bits

all the beer was poisoned and the capt. went down
and the mate and the cook
and we had nobody to grab sail
and the N.wester ripped the sheets like toenails
and we pitched like crazy
the hull tearing its sides
and all the time in the corner
some punk had a drunken slut (my wife)
and was pumping away
like nothing was happening
and the cat kept looking at me
and crawling in the pantry
amongst the clanking dishes
with flowers and vines painted on them
until I couldn't stand it anymore
and took the thing
and heaved it
over
the side.

Big Bastard with a Sword

listen, I went to get a haircut, it was a perfectly good day
until they brought it to me, I mean I sat waiting my turn in the
chair and I found a magazine—the usual thing: women with their
breasts hanging out, etc., and then I turned the page and here
were photos of Orientals in a field, there was a big
bastard with the sword—the caption said he had a very good
swing, plenty of power and the picture showed him getting ready
with the sword, and you saw an Oriental kneeling there with his
eyes closed, then—ZIP!—he was kneeling there without a head
and you could see the neck clean, not yet even
spurting blood, the separation having been so astonishingly
swift, and more photos of beheadings, and then a photo of these
heads lolling in the weeds without bodies, the sun shining on
  them.
and the heads looking still almost alive as if they hadn't
accepted the death—and then the barber said
                                next!

and I walked over to the chair and my head was still on
and his head said to my head,
           how do you want it?
           and I said, medium.

and he seemed like a nice sensible fellow
and it seemed nice to be near nice sensible fellows
and I wanted to ask him about the heads
but I thought it would upset him
or maybe even give him ideas
or he might say something that wouldn't help at
all
so I kept quiet.

I listened to him cut my hair
and he began talking about his baby
and I tried to concentrate on his

baby, it seemed very sane and logical
but I still kept thinking about the
heads.

when he finished the cutting
he turned me in the chair so I could look into the
mirror. my head was still on.

fine, I told him, and I got out of the chair, paid, and
gave him a good tip.

I walked outside and a woman walked by and she had her
head on and all the people driving cars had their heads
on.

I should have concentrated on the breasts, I thought,
it's so much better, all that hanging out, or
the magic and beautiful legs, sex was a fine thing
after all, but my day was spoiled, it would take a night's sleep
anyway, to get rid of the heads. it was terrible to be a human
being: there was so much going
on.

I saw my head in a plateglass window
I saw the reflection
and my head had a cigarette in it
my head looked tired and sad
it was not smiling with its new
haircut.

then
it disappeared
and I walked on
past the houses full of furniture and cats and
dogs and people
and they were lucky and I threw the cigarette
into the gutter
saw it burning on the asphalt

red and white, a tender spit of smoke,
and I decided that the sun
felt good.

About My Very Tortured Friend, Peter

he lives in a house with a swimming pool
and says the job is
killing him.
he is 27. I am 44. I can't seem to
get rid of
him. his novel keeps coming
back. "what do you expect me to do?" he screams
"go to New York and pump the hands of the
publishers?"
"no," I tell him, "but quit your job, go into a
small room and do the
thing."
"but I need ASSURANCE, I need something to
go by, some word, some sign!"
"some men did not think that way:
Van Gogh, Wagner—"
"oh hell, Van Gogh had a brother who gave him
paints whenever he
needed them!"

"look," he said, "I'm over at this broad's house today and
this guy walks in. a salesman. you know
how they talk. drove up in this new
car. talked about his vacation. said he went to
Frisco—saw *Fidelio* up there but forgot who
wrote it. now this guy is 54 years
old. so I told him: '*Fidelio* is Beethoven's only
opera.' and then I told
him: 'you're a jerk!' 'whatcha mean?' he
asked. 'I mean, you're a jerk, you're 54 years old and
you don't know anything!' "

"what happened
then?"
"I walked out."

"you mean you left him there with
her?"
"yes."

"I can't quit my job," he said. "I always have trouble getting a
job. I walk in, they look at me, listen to me talk and
they think right away, ah ha! he's too *intelligent* for
this job, he won't stay
so there's really no sense in hiring
him.
now, YOU walk into a place and you don't have any trouble:
you look like an old wino, you look like a guy who needs a
job and they look at you and they think:
ah ha!: now here's a guy who really needs work! if we hire
him he'll stay a long time and work
HARD!"

"do any of those people," he asks "know you are a
writer, that you write poetry?"
"no."
"you never talk about
it. not even to
me! if I hadn't seen you in that magazine I'd
have never known."
"that's right."
"still, I'd like to tell these people that you are a
writer!"
"don't."
"I'd still like to
tell them."
"why?"
"well, they talk about you. they think you are just a
horseplayer and a drunk."
"I am both of those."
"well, they talk about you. you have odd ways. you travel
   alone.
I'm the only friend you
have."

60

"yes."

"they talk you down. I'd like to defend you. I'd like to tell
them you write
poetry."

"leave it alone. I work here like they
do. we're all the same."

"well, I'd like to do it for *myself* then. I want them to know
   why
I travel with
you. I speak 7 languages, I know my music—"

"forget it."

"all right, I'll respect your
wishes. but there's something else—"

"what?"

"I've been thinking about getting a
piano. but then I've been thinking about getting a
violin too but I can't make up my
mind!"

"buy a piano."

"you think
so?"

"yes."

he walks away
thinking about
it.

I was thinking about it
too: I figure he can always come over with his
violin and more
sad music.

Not Quite So Soon

in the featherbeds of grander times
when Kings could call their shots,
I rather imagine on days like this
that concubines were sought,
or the unspoiled genius
or the chopping block.

how about a partridge or a grouse
or a bound behind the merry hounds?
Maybe I'll phone Saroyan in Malibu
or eat a slice of toast . . .

the trees shake down September
like dysentery, and churches sit on their
corners and wait, and the streetcars are slow,
and everywhere
birds fly, cats walk, people ruefully
exist . . .

the charmers are gone, the armies have put down
their arms, the druid's drunk, the horses have tossed
their dice; there are no fires, the phone won't ring,
the factory's closed, tenesmus, everything . . .

I think
even the schizomycetes are sleeping;
I think
the horror of no action is greater
than the scorch of pain; death is the
barker, but things
may get better
yet. I'll use the knives for spreading
jam, and the gas to warm
my greying love.

Counsel

as the wind breaks in from the sea again
and the land is marred with riot and disorder
be careful with the sabre of choice,
remember
what may have been noble
5 centuries
or even 20 years ago
is now
more often than not
wasted action
your life runs but once,
history has chance after chance
to prove men fools.

be careful, then, I would say,
of any seeming noble
deed
ideal
or action,
be for this country or love or Art,
be not taken by the nearness of the minute
or a beauty or politic
that will wilt like a cut flower;
love, yes, but not as a task of marriage,
and beware bad food and excessive labor;
live in a country, you must,
but love is not an order
either of woman or the land;
take your time; and drink as much as is needed
in order to maintain continuance,
for drink is a form of life
wherein the partaker returns to a new chance
at life; furthermore, I say,
live alone as much as possible;
bear children if it happens

but try not to bear
raising them; engage not in small arguments
of hand or voice
unless your foe seeks the life of your body
or the life of your soul; then,
kill, if necessary; and
when it comes time to die
do not be selfish:
consider it inexpensive
and where you are going:
neither a mark of shame or failure
or a call upon sorrow
as the wind breaks in from the sea
and time goes on
flushing your bones with soft peace.

I Wait in the White Rain

I wait in the white rain for knives like your tongue
I see the spiral clowns fountain up with myths untrue,
I wrestle spasms in the dark on dark stairways
while dollar crazy landladies
are threaded with the hot needles of sperm,
come these morning drunks
brushing away sunlight from the eyes like a web,
come darling, come gloria patri, come luck,
come anything,
this is the hot way—
points sticking in like armadillos
in the rear of a Benedictine mind,
and snow snow snow snow snow
shovel all the snow upon me I can hold,
gingerbread mouth, duck-like dick,
raisins for buttons, thread for heart-strings,
damned waves of blood caught in them
like a minnow in the Tide of Everywhere
I wait in the white rain for knives like your tongue,
and the trucks go by
with bankrupt faces
the steam of their essence like foul sweat
stale stink   death in my socks
all the drums of hell
cannot awaken a rhythm within me
I am gone
like an old pale goldfish
dead and stiff as aunt Helen
looking flat-eyed into the center of my brain
and flushed away like any other waste of man,
the man-turd, the breath of life,
and why we don't go mad as roaches, why not more
suicides I'll never know
as I wait in the white rain for knives like your tongue,
I am done, quite; like any ford that cuts off a river

I am done forever and only,
this christ-awful waiting on the end of a stale movie,
everyone screaming for beauty and victory
like children for candy,
my hands open
unamazed hand
unamazed mind
unamazed doorsill
send your flowers to Shakey Joe
or Butternut Carlyle
who might trade them to useful purpose
before everything, everyone,
is dead

Breakout

The landlord walks up and down the hall
coughing
letting me know he is there,
and I've got to sneak
in the bottles,
I can't walk to the crapper
the lights don't work,
there are holes in the walls from
broken water pipes
and the toilet won't flush,
and the little jackoff
walks up and down
out there
coughing, coughing,
up and down his faded rug
he goes,
and I can't stand it anymore,
I break out,
I GET him
just as he walks by,
"What the hell's wrong?"
he screams,
but it's too late,
my fist is working against the bone;
it's over fast and he falls,
withered and wet;
I get my suitcase and then
I am going down the steps,
and there's his wife in the doorway,
she's ALWAYS IN THE DOORWAY,
they don't have anything to do but
stand in doorways and walk up and down the halls,
"Good morning, Mr. Bukowski," her face is a mole's face
praying for my death, "what—"
and I shove her aside,

she falls down the porch steps and
into a hedge,
I hear the branches breaking
and I see her half-stuck in there
like a blind cow,
and then I am going down the street
with my suitcase,
the sun is fine,
and I begin to think about
the next place where I'm
going to set up, and I hope
I can find some decent humans,
somebody who can treat me
better.

I Cannot Stand Tears

there were several hundred fools
around the goose who broke her leg
trying to decide
what to do
when the guard walked up
and pulled out his cannon
and the issue was finished
except for a woman
who ran out of a hut
claiming he'd killed her pet
but the guard rubbed his straps
and told her
kiss my ass,
take it to the president;
the woman was crying
and I cannot stand tears.

I folded my canvas
and went further down the road:
the bastards had ruined
my landscape.

Horse on Fire

Bring bring
straight things
like a horse on fire

Ezra said,
write it
soaz a man on th' West Coast'a
Africka culd
understand ut;
and he proceeded to write the *Cantos*
full of dead languages
newspaper clippings
and love scenes from St. Liz;
bring bring
straight things: in bird-light,
the terror of a mouse,
grass-arms great stone heads;
and reading Canto 90
he put the paper down
Ez did (both their eyes were wet)
and he told her . . .
"among the greatest love poems
ever written."

Ezra, there are many kinds of traitors
of which
the political are the least,
but self-appraisal of
poetry and love
has proved more fools than
rebels.

Mother and Son

a lady in pink sits on her porch
in tight capris
and her ass is a marvelous thing
pink and crouched in the sun
her ass is a marvelous thing,
and now she rises and claps her hands
toward the sea
and shouts:
TIM, TIM, COME BACK, COME BACK
HERE! it is a child in a walker
running across the cement
looking for butterflies
and a way out,
and she chases him:
TIM, TIM, COME BACK HERE!
I watch her butt
her pink tight magic butt
and it rises in my mind
like a Beethoven symphony
but she is not mine.
I have been quietly reading about
the 18th century glass harmonica
and somebody else will take the pink wobble
to direct hand;
but
really
I've seduced her on this Sunday afternoon
and I have seen each movement and crawl
of pink flesh beneath pink capris,
and she catches her boy in the sun
and he laughs back at her
already a man on the dare
exploring the new front yards of his mind,
and he might resent that I have made love
to his mother   this way

71

as he might resent other things
later
pink red dawn blood bombs
the squealing of sheep
the taxis that ride us out,
or he might put on a necktie
choke out the mind
and become like the rest
therefore
making my pink love
upon these black keys
wasted.

The Day I Kicked Away a Bankroll

and, I said, you can take your rich aunts and uncles
and grandfathers and fathers
and all their lousy oil
and their seven lakes
and their wild turkey
and buffalo
and the whole state of Texas,
meaning, your crow-blasts
and your Saturday night boardwalks,
and your 2-bit library
and your crooked councilmen
and your pansy artists—
you can take all these
and your weekly newspaper
and your famous tornadoes,
and your filthy floods
and all your yowling cats
and your subscription to *Time,*
and shove them, baby,
shove them.

I can handle a pick and ax again (I think)
and I can pick up
25 bucks for a 4-rounder (maybe);
sure, I'm 38
but a little dye can pinch the gray
out of my hair;
and I can still write a poem (sometimes),
don't forget *that,* and even if
they don't pay off,
it's better than waiting for death and oil,
and shooting wild turkey,
and waiting for the world
to begin.

all right, bum, she said,
get out.

what? I said.

get out. you've thrown your
last tantrum.
I'm tired of your damned tantrums:
you're always acting like a
character in an O'Neill play.

but I'm different, baby,
I can't help
it.

you're different, all right!
God, how different!
don't slam
the door
when you leave.

but, baby, I *love* your
money!

you never once said
you loved me!

what do you want
a liar or a
lover?

you're neither! out, bum,
out!

. . . but baby!

go back to O'Neill!

74

I went to the door,
softly closed it and walked away,
thinking: all they want
is a wooden Indian
to say yes and no
and stand over the fire and
not raise too much hell;
but you're getting to be
an old man, kiddo;
next time play it closer
to the
vest.

The Dogs

certainly sought: one quiet time,
the horses of war
shot
with their broken legs,
air sprayed with the languor
of walking through a small neighborhood
at 6 p.m.
to smell porkchops frying,
the arrayed sensibility
of men living through light and sound,
and rain
if there be rain
or snow
if there be snow,
and pain,
living through wives and children
and the sensibility of fire
when it is cold; but
the dogs want a part of us,
they want all of us,
and coming in from the factory
to a bug-infected room
in East Kansas City
is not enough
(but who the enemy is
we are
not quite sure)
only
this morning
combing my hair
one eye on the clock,
wondering if another drink
would do,
I
think
I
saw them.

Imbecile Night

imbecile night,
corkscrew like a black guitar,
the day was heaving hell,
and now you come
crawling down the drainpipes
emptying your bladder
all over the place,
and I have drunk 9 bottles of beer,
a pint of vodka,
smoked 18 cigarettes,
and still you sit upon me,
you march the dead out upon
the balcony of my brain;
I see shaven eyebrows; lips, slippers;
my love, in an old robe, curses,
reaches out for me; the
Confederate Army runs; Hitler
turns a handspring . . . then
the yowling love of cats
saves me, brings me
back again . . . one more drink,
one more smoke, and in the drawer
a picture of a day at the beach
in 1955 . . . god, I was young then,
younger anyhow; and at the window,
one or 2 lights, the city is dead
except for thieves and janitors,
and I am almost dead too, so
much gone, and I raise the bottle
in the center of the room
and you are everywhere
black imbecile night,
you are under my fingernails,
in my ears and mouth,
and here we stand,

you and I, a giant and a midget
locked in disorder, and when the
first sun comes down showing the spiders
at work, caterpillars crawling on razor threads,
you will let me go,
but now you crawl into the tomb of my bottle,
you wink at me and posture, the wallpaper is
weak with roses, the spiders dream of
gold-filled flies, and I walk the room again,
light another cigarette, feeling I really
should go mad, but not quite knowing
how.

A Kind of Lecture on a Dull Day When There Isn't Even a Fly Around to Kill

don't kid yourself:
something kills them all—
finally it becomes a matter of
dying of one thing or
the other—
cancer, a new car, sex, warm
art, poetry, ballet dancing,
a hardware store, smoking grass, peeking
out of windows or
wiping the ass with
cheap toilet
paper

when Christ began
he had the cross in mind
all along.

if I came down off this one
here
it would only be to find a
better one.

meanwhile, sitting with a drink in hand
I know, of course,
what it's all
about, come to the point,
dismiss it, forget it,
hand to mouth
I kid myself a
little.

The Gift

that this is the gift
and I am ill with it;
it has sloshed around my bones
and brings me awake to
stare at walls.

musing often leads to madness,
o dog with an
old rag doll.

into and beyond terror.
seriousness will not do,
seriousness is gone:
we must carve from
fresh marble.

hell, jack, this is wise-time:
we must insist on camouflage,
they taught us that;
wine come down through
staring eye,
god coughed alive
through the indistinct smoke
of verse.

the light yellow mamas are gone
the garter high on the leg,
the charm of 18 is 80.
and the kisses,
snakes darting liquid silver
have stopped:
no man lives the magic
long.

until one morning it catches you;
you light the fire,
pour a hasty drink
as the psyche crawls like a mouse
into an empty pantry.

if you were El Greco
or even a watersnake
something could be done.

another drink.
well, rub your hands
and prove you are alive.
walk the floor. seriousness
will not do.

this is the gift,
this is the gift . . .
certainly the charm of dying
lies in the fact
that very little
is lost.

Object Lesson

It is always best, of course,
to push it in right below
the heart.

Don't try to hit the
bull's eye.

When seeking damage
aim for a large target
and strike several times.

He who pauses is
one damn fool.

I remember a discourse
with a leper
who suggested using
hooks and pulleys.

Not so. Not so.

He was very bitter.

It is best to go for the eye,
smash the cornea,
blind him,
then strangle him with rope.

My mother suggested an old bathing cap
down the throat.

Not so. Not so.

Be safe. Be wise.

Tell him to seek the stars
and he will kill himself with climbing.

Tell him about Chatterton. Villon.

Make suggestions.
Take your time.
He will do it himself.

There is no hurry. Time means nothing
to you.

Goldfish

my goldfish stares with watery eyes
into the hemisphere of my sorrow;
upon the thinnest of threads
we hang together,
hang hang hang
in the hangman's noose;
I stare into his place and
he into mine . . .
he must have thoughts,
can you deny this?
he has eyes and hunger
and his love too
died in January; but he is
gold, really gold, and I am grey
and it is indecent to search him out,
indecent like the burning of peaches
or the rape of children,
and I turn and look elsewhere,
but I know that he is there behind me,
one gold goblet of blood,
one thing alone
hung between the reddest cloud
of purgatory
and apt. no. 303.

god, can it be
that we are the same?

Sleep

she was a short one
getting fat and she had once been
beautiful and
she drank the wine
she drank the wine in bed and
talked and screamed and cursed at
me
and i told her
>   please, I need some
>   sleep.

>   —sleep? sleep? you son of a
>   bitch, you never sleep, you
>   don't need any
>   sleep!

I buried her one morning early
I carried her down the sides of the Hollywood Hills
brambles and rabbits and rocks
running in front of me
and by the time I'd dug the ditch
and stuck her in
belly down
and put the dirt back on
the sun was up and it was warm
and the flies were lazy and
I could hardly see anything out of my eyes
everything was so
warm and yellow.

I managed to drive home and I got into bed and I
slept for 5 days and 4
nights.

Hello, Willie Shoemaker

the Chinaman said don't take the hardware
and gave me a steak I couldn't cut (except the fat)
and there was an ant circling the coffee cup;
I left a dime tip and broke out a stick of cancer,
and outside I gave an old bum who looked about
the way I felt, I gave him a quarter,
and then I went up to see the old man
strong as steel girders, fit for bombers and blondes,
up the green rotten steps that housed rats
and past the secretaries showing leg and doing nothing
and the old man sat there looking at me
through two pairs of glasses and a vacation in Paris,
and he said, Kid, I hear you been takin' Marylou out,
and I said, just to dinner, boss,
and he said, just to dinner, eh? you couldn't hold
that broad's pants on with all the rivets on 5th street,
and please remember you are a shipping clerk,
I am the boss here and I pay these broads and I pay you.
yes, sir, I said, and I felt he was going to skip it
but he slid my last check across the desk
and I took it and walked out
past
all the lovely legs, the skirts pulled up to the ass,
Marylou's ass, Ann's ass, Vicki's ass, all of them,
and I went down to the bar
and George said whatya gonna do now,
and I said go to Russia or Hollywood Park,
and I looked up in time to see Marylou come in,
the long thin nose, the delicate face, the lips, the legs,
the breasts, the music, the talk the love the laughing
and she said
I quit when I found out
and the bastard got down on his knees and cried
and kissed the hem of my skirt and offered me money
and I

walked out
and he blubbered like a baby.
George, I said, another drink, and I put a quarter in
the juke
and the sun came out
and I looked outside in time to see the old bum
with my quarter
and a little more luck
that had turned into a happy wine-bottle,
and a bird even flew by *cheep cheep,*
right there on Eastside downtown, no kidding,
and the Chinaman came in for a quickie
claiming somebody had stolen a spoon and a coffee cup
and I leaned over and bit Marylou on the ear
and the whole joint rocked with music and freedom
and I decided that Russia was too far away
and Hollywood Park just close enough.

There is this long still knife somehow like a
cossack's sword . . .

    and C. writes that Ferlinghetti has written
    a poem about Castro. well, all the boys
    are doing poems on Castro now, only
    Castro's not that good
    or that bad—just a small horse
    in a big race.

I see this knife on the stove and I move it to
the breadboard . . .

    after a while it is time to look around and
    listen to the engines and wonder if it's
    raining; after a while writing won't help
    anymore, and drinking won't help anymore, or
    even a good piece of ass won't.

I see this knife on the breadboard and I move it
to the sink . . .

    this wallpaper here: how many years was it here
    before I arrived? . . . this cigarette in my hand
    it is like a thing itself, like a donkey walking
    uphill . . . somebody took my candle and candle-
    holder: a lady with red hair and a white face
    standing near the closet, saying, "Can I have
    this? can I really have this?"

The edge of the knife is not as sharp as it should
be . . . but the point, the point fascinates, the way
they grind it down like that—symmetry, real Art,
and I pick up this breadknife and walk into the
dining room . . .

Larsen says we mustn't take ourselves so
seriously. Hell, I've been telling him that
for 8 years!

There is this full length mirror in the hall. I
can see myself in it and I look, at last.
It hasn't rained in 175 days and it
is as quiet as a sleeping peacock. a
friend of mine shoots pool in a hall across from
the university where he teaches English, and when
he gets tired of that, he drags out a .357 magnum
and splits the rocks in half BLAM! BLAM! BLAM!
while figuring just where the word will fit real
good. In front of the mirror I cut swift circles in the
air, dividing sides of light. I am hypnotized,
unsettled, embarrassed. my nose is pink, my
cheeks are pink, my throat is white, the phone
rings like a wall sliding down and I answer
"Nothing, no, I'm not doing anything . . ."

it is a dull conversation but it is soon over. I
walk to the window and open it. the cars go by
and a bird turns on the wire and looks at me. I
think 3 centuries ahead, of myself dead that long
and life seems very odd . . . like a crack of
light in a buried tomb.

the bird flies away and I walk to the machine and
sit down:

Dear Willie:

I got your letter, everything fine
here . . .

Countryside

I drive my car
through a valley
where
(very oddly)
young girls sit on fencerails
showing impartial leg and
haunch
in butterglory sun,
young girls painting
cows and
trees in heat
painting
old farms that sit like
pools of impossibility
on unplanted ground,
ground as still and insane
as the weathervanes
stuck northwest
in the degenerate air;
I drive on
with the girls and their brushes and
their taffy bodies stuck inside my
       head like
toothache,
and I get out
much farther down the road
walk into a peeling white cafe
and am handed water in a glass as
       thick as a
lip, and
4 people sit
eating,
eyes obsessed with molecules of no
urgency;
I order a veal cutlet and the

waitress walks away
trussed in white flat linen
and I sit and watch and wait
so disattached I wish I could
cry or curse or break the water glass;
instead I pour cream into the
coffee
I think of the girls and the cows,
stir the cream with a damaged and
        apologetic
tinkle
then decide
not to think or feel anymore
that day.

Death Wants More Death

death wants more death, and its webs are full:
I remember my father's garage, how child-like
I would brush the corpses of flies
from the windows they had thought were escape—
their sticky, ugly, vibrant bodies
shouting like dumb crazy dogs against the glass
only to spin and flit
in that second larger than hell or heaven
onto the edge of the ledge,
and then the spider from his dank hole
nervous and exposed
the puff of body swelling
hanging there
not really quite knowing,
and then *knowing*—
something sending it down its string,
the wet web,
toward the weak shield of buzzing,
the pulsing;
a last desperate moving hair-leg
there against the glass
there alive in the sun,
spun in white;

and almost like love:
the closing over,
the first hushed spider-sucking:
filling its sack
upon this thing that lived;
crouching there upon its back
drawing its certain blood
as the world goes by outside
and my temples scream
and I hurl the broom against them:
the spider dull with spider-anger

still thinking of its prey
and waving an amazed broken leg;
the fly very still,
a dirty speck stranded to straw;
I shake the killer loose
and he walks lame and peeved
towards some dark corner
but I intercept his dawdling
his crawling like some broken hero,
and the straws smash his legs
now waving
above his head
and looking
looking for the enemy
and somehow valiant,
dying without apparent pain
simply crawling backward
piece by piece
leaving nothing there
until at last the red gut-sack splashes
its secrets,
and I run child-like
with God's anger a step behind,
back to simple sunlight,
wondering
as the world goes by
with curled smile
if anyone else
saw or sensed my crime.

Eat

talking of death
is like talking of
money—
we neither know the
price or the
worth,
yet looking down at my hands
I can guess
a little.

man's made for guessing and for
failure
and woman
for the rest.

when the time comes
I hope I can remember
eating a pear.

we are sick now
with so many dead
dogs
skulls
armies
flowers
continents.

there is a fight—

this is it:
against the mechanics
of the thing.

eat a good pear today
so tomorrow

**you can
remember
it.**

10 Lions and
the End of the World

in a national magazine of repute
(yes, I was reading it)
I saw a photograph of lions
crossing a street
in some village
and taking their time;
that's the way
it should be
and some day when
they turn out the lights
and the whole thing's over,
I'll be sitting here
in the chalky smoke
thinking of those 10 damned
(yes, I counted them)
lions
blocking traffic
while the roses bloomed.
we all ought to
do that
now
while there's
t
i
m
e.

The Blackbirds Are Rough Today

lonely as a dry and used orchard
spread over the earth
for use and surrender.

shot down like an ex-pug selling
dailies on the corner.

taken by tears like
an aging chorus girl
who has gotten her last check.

a hanky is in order your lord your
worship.

the blackbirds are rough today
like
ingrown toenails
in an overnight
jail—
wine wine whine,
the blackbirds run around and
fly around
harping about
Spanish melodies and bones.

and everywhere is
nowhere—
the dream is as bad as
flapjacks and flat tires:

why do we go on
with our minds and
pockets full of
dust
like a bad boy just out of

school—
you tell
me,
you who were a hero in some
revolution
you who teach children
you who drink with calmness
you who own large homes
and walk in gardens
you who have killed a man and own a
beautiful wife
you tell me
why I am on fire like old dry
garbage.

we might surely have some interesting
correspondence.
it will keep the mailman busy.
and the butterflies and ants and bridges and
cemeteries
the rocket-makers and dogs and garage mechanics
will still go on a
while
until we run out of stamps
and/or
ideas.

don't be ashamed of
anything; I guess God meant it all
like
locks on
doors.

A Word on the Quick and Modern Poem-Makers

it is quite easy to appear modern
while in reality being the biggest damnfool
                                    ever born;
I know: I have gotten away with some awful stuff
but not nearly such awful pot as I read in the journals;
I have an honesty self-born of whores and hospitals
that will not allow me to pretend to be
something which I am not—
which is a double failure: the failure of people
in poetry
and the failure of people
in life.
and when you fail in poetry
you fail life,
and when you fail life
you were never born
no matter what the statistics
or what your mother named you.

the grandstands are crowded with the dead
screaming for a winner
wanting a number to carry them over
into living,
but it is not as easy as that—
just as with the poem:
if you are dead
you might as well be buried
and throw the typewriter away
and stop fooling with
poems   horses   women   life:
you are cluttering up
the exits—
so get out fast
and desist from the
precious few
pages.

Seahorse

I own the ticks on a horse
I own his belly and balls
I own this
the way his eyes roll
the way he eats hay
and shits and
stands up asleep

he is mine
this machine
like a blue train I used to play with
when my hands were smaller
and my mind better

I own this horse,
someday I will ride my horse
down all the streets
past the trees we will go
up the mountain
down the valley

ticks and eyes and balls
the both of us
we will go to where kings eat
dandelions
in the giant sea
where thinking is not terror
where eyes do not go out
like Saturday night children

the horse I own and the myself I own
will become blue and nice and clean
again

and I will get off and
wait for you.

I Have Lived in England

I have lived in England
and I have lived in hell,
but perhaps there is nothing quite so horrible
as picking up the latest literary review
filled with the latest literary darlings;
K. teaches at L.; M. has a second volume of
poems coming out; O. has been published
in the leading journals; S. has won a
scholarship to Paris—

and you hold the pages up
to the overhead light
and still
          nothing comes through.

it is a puzzle indeed,
far more a puzzle than when a 90-to-one shot
leaps through at the last moment
along the rail.

a horse can live.

and, indeed, do you expect to find
poetry
in a poetry review?

things are not that
simple.

Farewell, Foolish Objects

I have lain in bed all day
but I have written one poem
and I am up now
looking out the window
and like a novelist might say
drunk: the clouds are coming at me
like scullery maids with dishpans
in their hands—
something that holds gritty dirty
water.
but I am a drunken non-novelist
but in clear condition now
here sits the bottle of beer
and I am warmly thinking
in a kind of foam-shaped idle fancy
working closely
but all I can stoke up are
squares and circles which
do not fit; so
messeigneurs
I will tell you the truth:
again (in bed)
I read another article on D. Thomas &
some day I will get lucky and sit around
and own a French horn and a tame eagle
and I will sit on the porch all day
a white porch always in the sun
one of those white porches with green
vines all around, and
I will *read* about Dylan and D.H. until
my eyes fall out of my head for eagle
meat and I will play the French horn
blind. but even now it gets darker
the evening thing into night
the bones down here

the stars up there
somebody rattling the springs in
Denver so another pewker can be born.
I think everything is a sheet of sun
and the best of everything
is myself walking through it
wondering about the pure *nerve*
of the life-thing going on:
after the jails the hospitals
the factories the good dogs
the brainless butterflies.
but now I am back at the window
there is an opera on the radio
and a woman sits in a chair to my left
saying over and over again:
BRATCH BRATSHT BRAATCHT!
and she is holding a book in her hand:
How to Learn Russian Easily.
but there is really nothing you can do
easily: live or die or accept fame
or money or defeat, it's all hard.
the opera says this, the dead birds
the dead countries the dead loves
the man shot because somebody thought
he was an elk
the elk shot because somebody thought
it was an elk.
all the pure *nerve* of going on
this woman wanting to speak Russian
myself wanting to get drunk
but we need something to eat.
GRIND CAT GRIND MEAT says
the woman in Russian so I figure
she's hungry, we haven't eaten
in a couple of hours. CLAM
BAYONET TURKEY PORK
AND PORK she says, and I walk
over and put on my pants and

I am going out to get something.
the forests are far away and I am
no good with the bow and arrow
and somebody sings on the radio:
"farewell, foolish objects."
and all I can do is walk into a grocery
store and pull out a wallet and hope
that it's loaded. and this is
about how I waste my Sundays.
the rest of the week gets better
because there is somebody telling
me what to do
and although it seems madness
almost everybody is doing it
whatever it is.
so now if you will excuse me
(she is eating an orange now)
I will put on my shoes and shirt
and get out of here—it'll
be better for
all of us.

A Report Upon the Consumption of Myself

I am a panther shut up and bellowing in
cement walls, and I am angry at blue
evenings without ventilation
and I am angry with you, and it will come
                                        like a rose
it will come like a man walking through fire
it will shine like an unseen trumpet in a trunk
the eyes will smell like sausages
the feet will have small propellers
and I will hold you in Bayonne and
the sailors will smile
my heart like something cut away from
cancer will feel and beat again feel
and beat again—but now
the blue evening is cinched like old
muskets and the dangling sex rope hangs
as the tree stands up and calls:
July. the dust of hope in the bottom of paper cups
along with small spiders that have names like ancient
European cities; spit and dross, heavy wheels;
oilwells stuck between fish and sucking up the grey gas
of love and the palms up on the cliff waving
waving in the warm yellow light
as I walk into a drugstore to buy toothpaste,
rubbers, photographs of frogs, a copy of the latest
Consumer Reports (50 cents) for I consume and
am consumed and would like to know
on this blue evening
just which razorblade it would be best for me
to use, or maybe I could get a station wagon or buy a
stereo or a movie camera, say 8mm, under $55
or an electric frying pan . . . like the silver head
of some god-thing after they drop the bomb *BANG*
and the grass gives up and love is a shadow
and love is a fishtail weaving through

threads that seem eyes but are only what's
left of me on the last blue evening after the bands
have suicided out, the carnival has left town and
they've blown up the Y.W.C.A. like a giant balloon and
sent it out to sea full of screaming lovely lonely
girls.

Fleg

Now it's Borodin . . . 4:18 a.m.,
symphony *#2*,
the gas is on
but the masses still sleep
except the bastard
downstairs
who always has the light on
all night, he yawns all night
and sleeps all day,
he's either a madman
or a poet; and has an
ugly wife,
neither of them work
and we pass each other
on the steps (the wife and I)
when we go down
to dump our bottles,
and I look at his name
on the mailbox: *Fleg*
God. *No wonder.* A fleg
never sleeps. Some kind
of fish-thing waiting
for a twist in the sky.
but very kind, I must
remember, when the
drunk women up here
scream or throw things
Fleg ignores it all,
yawns, and this is
fine. There used to be
an *Anderson,* a *Chester
Anderson* always at my door
in his pants
and undershirt,
red-eyed as a woman

who has lost a lover,
manager behind his shoulder
(and one night 2 cops),
"God, I can't *sleep*.
I'm a *working* man,
I've got to get my *sleep*
Jesus. I can't SLEEP."

Fleg? *Sleep*? I've never even
seen him. I don't think
he does *anything*. Just some
kind of shoulder of mutton
with silver eyes
looking up at his ceiling,

tiredly smiling,
saying softly to his
ugly wife: "That *Bukowski*
up there, he's a kick
for sore balls, ain't he?"

"Now, Honey, don't talk that way."

"He had a colored woman up there
the other night. I can tell,
I can tell."

"Now, Mission, you can't tell no
such damn thing."

(*Mission*? *Mission Fleg*. Christ.)

"Yes, I can. I heard her screaming."

"Screaming?"

"Well, moaning, kind of like you
know. What's this guy look like,
baby?"

"Passed him today. Face kind of smashed
in. A long nose like an ant-eater.
Mouth like a monkey. Kind of funny eyes.
Never saw eyes like those."

It's about 4:38 a.m. Borodin is finished (yeah)
not a very long symphony. I turn my radio down
and the Flegs I find
are listening
to the same station.

I hope we never meet,
I like Fleg the way he is
(in my mind)
and I'm sure he wants me
the way I am
(in his mind),
and he has just yawned now
up through the ceiling
his ceiling
which is my floor; ah,
my *poor tired* Fleg
waiting for me to give
him LIFE;
he's probably slowly dying of
something
and I am too,
but I'm so glad
he doesn't call the police
while I'm
at it.

this South American up here on a Gugg
walked in with his whore
and she sat on the edge of my bed and
crossed her fine legs
and I kept looking at her legs
and he pulled at his stringy necktie
and I had a hangover
and he asked me
WHAT DO YOU THINK OF THE AMERICAN
POETS?
and I told him I didn't think very much
of the American poets
and then he went on to ask some other
very dull questions
(as his whore's legs layed along the side of
my brain) like
WELL? YOU DON'T CARE ABOUT ANYTHING
BUT IF YOU WERE TEACHING A CLASS AND ONE OF THE
STUDENTS ASKED YOU WHICH AMERICAN POETS
THEY SHOULD READ
WHAT WOULD YOU TELL THEM?
she crossed her legs as I watched and I thought
I could knock him out with one punch
rape her in 4 minutes
catch a train for L.A.
get off in Arizona and walk off into the desert
and I couldn't tell him that I would never teach
a class
that along with not liking American poetry
that I didn't like American classes either
or the job that they would expect me to
do,
so I said
Whitman, T. S. Eliot, D. H. Lawrence's poems about
reptiles and beasts, Auden. and then I

110

realized that Whitman was the only true American,
that Eliot was not an American somehow and the
others certainly not, and
he knew it too
he knew that I had fucked up
but I made no apologies
thought some more about rape
I almost loved the woman but I knew that when she walked out
that I would never see her again
and we shook hands and the Gugg said
he'd send me the article when it came out
but I knew that he didn't have an article
and he knew it too
and then he said
I will send you some of my poems translated into
English
and I said fine
and I watched them walk out of the place
I watched her highheels clack down the tall
green steps
and then both of them were gone
but I kept remembering her dress sliding all over her
like a second skin
and I was wild with mourning and love and sadness
and being a fool unable to
communicate
anything
and I walked in and finished that beer
cracked another
put on my ragged king's coat
and walked out into the New Orleans street
and that very night
I sat with my friends and acted vile and
the ass
much mouth and villainy
and cruelness
and they never
knew why.

Very

I take the taxi to Newport and study the wrinkles in the
driver's skull; all anticipation is gone:
defeat has come so often
(like rain)
that it has assumed more meaning
than victory; the player is good at
the piano
and we wait in a corner
(this poet!)
waiting to recite
poems; it's like a cave here:
full of bats and whores
and bodiless music
moving at the back of the world; my head aches,
and seeking a deliberate door
I think gently of successful papa Haydn
rotting in the rainy garden
above copulating
tone-deaf gophers . . .

the sun is in a box somewhere
asleep like a cat;
                    the bats flit, a body
takes my hand (the one with the drink:
the right hand is the drinker)
    a woman, a horrible
    damned woman,
    something alive
    sits
    and blinks
    at me:
Hank, it says,
they want you up
    front!
fuck 'em, I say, fuck 'em.

I have grown quite fat and
vulgar (a deliberate death
on the kitchen floor) and
suddenly I laugh
at my excellent condition
like some swine of a businessman
and I don't even feel
like getting up
to piss . . .

    Angels,
we have grown apart.

The Look:

I once bought a toy rabbit
at a department store
and now he sits and ponders
me with pink sheer eyes:

He wants golfballs and glass
walls.
I want quiet thunder.

Our disappointment sits between us.

One Night Stand

the latest sleeping on my pillow catches
window lamplight through the mist of alcohol.

I was the whelp, the prude who shook when
the wind shook blades of grass the eye could see
and
you were a
convent girl watching the nuns shake loose
the Las Cruces sand from God's robes

you are
yesterday's
bouquet so sadly
raided, I kiss your poor
breasts as my hands reach for love
in this cheap Hollywood apartment smelling of
bread and gas and misery.

we move through remembered routes
the same old steps smooth with hundreds of
feet, 50 loves, 20 years.
and we are granted a very small summer, and
then it's
winter again
and you are moving across the floor
some heavy awkward thing
and the toilet flushes, a dog barks
a car door slams . . .
it's gotten inescapably away, everything,
it seems, and I light a cigarette and
await the oldest curse
of all.

Poem to a Most Affectionate Lady

Please keep your icecream hands
for the leopard,
please keep your knees
out of my nuts;
if women must love me
I ask them also
to cook me sauerkraut dinners
and leave me time
for games of gold
in the mind,
and time for sleep
or scratching
or rolling upon my side
like any tired bull
in any tired meadow.

love is not a candle
burning down—
life is,
and love and life are
not the same
or else
love having choice
nobody would ever die.

which means? which means:
let loose a moment
your hand upon my center—
I've done you well
like any scrabby plant
upon a mountain, so
please be kind enough
to die for an hour
or 2,
or at least

take time
to turn the
sauerkraut.

Parts of an Opera, Parts of a Guitar,
Part of Nowhere

I don't know, it was raining and I had fallen down
somewhere but I seemed to have money so it didn't
matter, and I went into the opera to dry off, and it
was opening night and everybody was dressed and
trying
to act very polite and educated but I saw a lot of
guys there mean as hell, I don't mean mean enough
to be
a Dillinger but mean enough to be successful in
business and their wives were all tone deaf
and even the people hollering in the opera
were not enjoying it but hollering because it was the
thing to do, like wearing bermudas in the summer, and
I thought, I'll never write an opera because they'll
walk all over it, and I walked out
and phoned a gal I knew from South Philly and she met
me on Olvera Street and we went into a fancy place
and ate and drank and this big female kept
whirling her fans and shaking her ass in my face
and the South Philly broad got mad and I laughed
and a little Mexican mean as a tarantula
kept asking us to keep quiet and I asked him out
in the alley and he went and I took him quite
easily and I felt like Hemingway and I took the
S. Philly broad to my room and I told her all about
the opera
              how the people were so nicely dressed
              and applauded all the time
              whether it was good or bad
and we slept real good that night
the rain coming down on our heads
through the open window
but I kept thinking of the bigassed Mexican gal
with the fans who kept shaking it

118

and I don't think she was kidding
because I am real handsome
and educated
and someday I'm going to give up
drinking and smoking and whoring
and kneel and pray in the Sunday sunshine
while they are killing the beautiful bulls
and selling their ears and tails in
Tiajuana, and I'm going to the opera,
I'm going to the opera and have 12 guys
working for me for
80 dollars a week, including half-days on
Saturdays and no
hangovers on
Monday.

Letter from the North

my friend writes of rejection and editors,
and how he has visited K. or R. or W.,
and am I in *S.#12*? he will have a poem in there,
and T. has written him from Florida
but rejected his poems; R. sleeps in the printshop
and T. chided him mercilessly . . .
met editor of the *X. Review* in the street,
and editor acted like he was kicked in the nuts
when he found out who he was
and pressed him for opinion of poems;
it does good to corner these guys sometime,
flush them outa the brush;
ad agencies have forgotten him, and W. is taking
too long to read his book; only got $5
for reading at the Unicorn,
phoned K. of the *W. Review,* sounds like a sharp guy;
and he thinks he is done with R.;
encloses some clippings for my amusement:
his name in a newspaper column;
he'll have to call R. again: S. is lecturing at
the university
and he can't bear to go; M. is a homo,
C. can't make up his mind and P. is mad at him
because he drank beer in front of N.
nothing but rejects but he knows his stuff is good.
L. was there to borrow a pack of Pall Malls, bastard makes
him sick, always whining . . .
B. writes that P. is in trouble, they must organize
a benefit;
awful discouraged. not even money for stamps.
dead without stamps. write me, he says,
I got the blues.

write you? about what, my friend?
I'm only interested in
poetry.

The Best Way to Get Famous
Is to Run Away

I found a loose cement slab outside the icecream store,
tossed it aside and began to dig; the earth was
soft and full of worms and soon I was in to my
waist, size 36;
a crowd gathered but stepped back before my shots
of mud,
and by the time the police came, I was in below
my head,
frightening gophers, eels and finding bits of golden
inlaid skull,
and they asked me, are you looking for oil, treasure,
gold, the end of China? are you looking for love, God,
a lost key chain? and little girls dripping icecream
peered into my darkness, and a psychiatrist came
and a
college professor and a movie actress in a bikini, and
a Russian spy and a French spy and an English spy,
and a drama critic and a bill collector and an old
girl friend, and they all asked me, what are you
looking
for? and soon it began to rain . . . atomic submarines
changed course, Tuesday Weld hid behind a newspaper,
Jean-Paul Sartre rolled in his sleep, and my hole
filled
with water; I came out black as Africa, shooting
stars
and epitaphs, my pockets full of lovely worms,
and they took me to their jail and gave me a shower
and a nice cell, rent-free, and even now the people
are picketing in my cause, and I have signed
contracts to appear on the stage and television,
to write a guest column for the local paper and
write a book and endorse some products, I have
enough money to last me several years at the best

121

hotels, but as soon as I get out of here, I'm gonna find me another loose slab and begin to dig, dig, dig, and this time I'm not coming back . . . rain, shine, or bikini, and the reporters keep asking, why did you do it? but I just light my cigarette and smile . . .

The Kings Are Gone

to say great words of kings and life
to give equations like a math genius;
I sat in on a play by Shakespeare,
but the grandeur did not come through;
I do not claim to have a good ear
or a good soul, but most of Shakespeare
laid me dry, I confess,
and I went me into a bar
where a man with hands like red crabs
laid his sick life before me through the fumes,
and I grew drunk,
mirror upon myself,
the age of life like a spider
taking last blood from us all,
and I knew I had misjudged Shakey,
his voice speaking out of the tube of the grave,
and the traffic went past
I could see it out the door,
pieces of things that moved
and the red crab hands moved before my face
and I took my drink then knocked it over
with the back of my hand;
and I walked out on the street
but nothing got better.

Reprieve and Admixture

exposed to grief too long
I become in time
surfeited with suffering,
decide that I owe myself
survival; this is not easy:
telling yourself that you
deserve better days
after the history of your past;
but I have seen complete fools
go on (of course)
without ever
considering their shortcomings;
then too turtles crawl the
land, dirty words scratched
on their backs . . .
but they hardly
improve the horizon.

The Swans Walk My Brain
in April It Rains

would you have me peel an orange and
talk of Saavedra (Miguel de) Cervantes?
get out! you are like that fly on the
curtain.

I am not liked in the marketplace.
I do not smile at the children.
I am not interested in the doings of
armies.
I drink at fountains until my eyes
stick out like ripe berries.
I stink under the armpits and do not
shine my shoes.
I do not own
anything.

I understand little but my
misuse.
I understand only horror and
more horror.

I cannot rhyme.
I am too tired to
steal.
I listen to Segovia
smile.
I look at a hog's head and
am in
love.

I walk I walk a
hymenotomy of a
man—o
sweet things of this time
where are you?

you must find me now for I am
terrified with what I
see!

the dungeons sweep past lit with
eyes. eyes? *magma!*
I enter a shop and buy wine from a
dead man
then walk away under a sky overflowing
with pus. the hunters cough
on the benches.

I walk . . .

The End

here they come
grey and beastly
rubbing out the night
with their bloodred torches,
Numbo! they scream,
Hail Numbo!
and grocer John gets down
on the floor and hugs
his precious eggs
and sausage,
and the bats of
Babe Ruth get up and
strut their
averages
around a dark bar,
and the grey blonde in bed
with me asks
"what's all the noise?"
and I say,
"the world is coming
to an end."
and we sit in the window
and watch, strangely
happy. we have 14 cigarettes
and a bottle of wine.
enough to last
until they
find us.

A Farewell Thing While Breathing

a farewell thing while breathing
was walking down the hall
in underwear
with painted face like clown
a bomb from Cologne in right pocket
a *Season in Hell*
in the left,
stripes of sunset
like
bass
running
down
his
arms,
and they found him in the morning
dangling in the fire escape
window,
face frosted and gone as an electric bulb,
and the sparrows
were in the brush downstairs,
and
friend,
sparrows do not sing
and they
(the people, not the sparrows)
carried him down the steps
like a wasted owl.

Sad-Eyed Mules of Men

daily the
sledgehammers and the
sad-eyed mules of men, &
there was Christ hung like
dried bacon, and now
the con-men raking it in:
the young girls
the mansions
the trips to
Paris, and look:
even the great artists
the great writers
raking it in.
but where do we go
while the great writers are
saving their own
souls?
where do we go?
. . . to hell, of course, juggling their
collected works
under our
collective
arms.

this
is what happens when the
drink and the life
catch up with what is left of
one.
I still hope to send you the
paperback although it is all
swollen.

I read
most of it in the bathroom where the
faucets drip hot water and make
steam
and that is what happened to the pages and
the binding is about to
pop
but I still thought I'd mail it to
you but
something always interferes—

there is a mirror
                    here and
I see myself in the mirror
and I stagger like a deer taking a
slug in the neck

the face is not what it should
be and I tell myself that it does not
matter
that I
am tired of factual and recognized
good
that we need new goodness new
truth for
ourselves and

let the others wear that
out.

but anyhow
I still hope to mail you the
paperback
I am sure I will mail it to you
sometime I think I will
just walk into the room and brush by
knock it to the floor with my
hand and pick it up
without looking at anything
and I will find an envelope and
mail it to
you.

I want to get it out
of here.

A Conversation on Morality,
Eternity and Copulation

all up and down the street they came back
without arms or legs or eyes or
lungs or minds or
lives, although
the war had been
won
and the madam stood in the doorway
and told me,
it won't matter, it'll be
business as
usual
because if they haven't shot off
the other parts
they'll still want to
fuck.

and the dead? I
asked.

the dead are without money or
sense.

many of the living are the same
way? I suggested.

yeah, but those we don't
serve.

God will love
you.

I'm sure He
will.

will you serve
Him?

I have been serving Him, you know
that: men are men and
soldiers are soldiers and
they love to
fuck, don't
you?

amen, I
said.

133

Soirée

ants crawl upon paper flowers with all the insect color
of my hatred and
I crash out the lamp and rise to scream,
but, lo, I am greater than garlic and faster
than the foreigner Errico!

in the cupboard sits my bottle
like a dwarf waiting to scratch out my prayers.
I drink and cough like some idiot at a symphony,
sunlight and maddened birds are everywhere,
the phone rings gamboling its sound
against the odds of the crooked sea;
I drink deeply and evenly now,
I drink to paradise
and death
and the lie of love.

at the window I watch the soldiers parachute down
as my radio plays the *Symphonie Fantastique* by
Berlioz;
the lightning stills the ants, stiffens them with
the fear of man, and there is a knock upon my door.
I walk with my luger and turn the knob. everything
is nonsense, nothing matters. the flies are upon
the sugar, wildly in the small richness: they have
my blithe and tinkered soul . . .

THE MARCH TO THE GALLOWS!

I laugh gaily as the chandeliers swing
and the last of the lovers
clutch at the straws of their lives,
and I fire through the doorway
as the music sinks to a lisp at the dismay
and derangement
of Birth.

Notations from a Muddled Indolence

a woman walks by and I look at her and know that her
   existence is
depleted of thought and worms
that she does not realize that successful men can be such
beasts
that she does not know that I have fallen into the sloth of
formula

I watch her as I sit in a dirty kitchen on a dirty
afternoon
she walks dreaming of oranges and
Cadillacs

mentally I throw her up into a palm
tree
physically I rape her
spiritually I spit in her
eye

I realize that really she is no more say than
some words written by a small boy in a public
crapper

these innumerable and astounding
realizations
this dirty
life

her skin is white and sagging
she has on a purple
underslip

this is what causes
wars
great paintings

suicides
harps
geognosy and
hermits.

Nothing Subtle

there is nothing subtle about dying or
dumping garbage, or the spider
and this fist full of nickels and
the barking of dogs tonight
when the beast puffs on beer
and moonlight,
and asks my name
and I hold to the wall
not man enough to cry
as the city dumps its sorrow
in wine bottles and stale kisses,
and the handcuffs and crutches and slabs
fornicate like mad.

I Don't Need a Bedsheet with
Slits for Eyes to Kill You in

if it's raining and you're sitting behind a shade with
a cup of curari or a dead
antelope
with bluer eyes than any of the beautiful blue eyes
of any of the girls in this ugly
town
I'll paint your fence green or
unplug your drain for almost
nothing;
if the fog comes in like soft cleanser
and you can see old men looking out at it
from behind curtains
these warm old men smoking pipes
I will tell you stories to make your dreams
easier;
but if you mutilate me
hang me alongside the scarecrow like a
cheap Christ
and let some schoolboy hang a sign about my
throat
I'm going to walk your streets of night
with a knife
in the rain in the snow
on gay holidays I'll be there
behind you
and when I decide finally that we will
meet
you will not understand
because you did not want
to
and the flowers and the dogs and the
cities and the children will not
miss you.

138

the most binding labor
is
trying to make it
under a sanctified
banner.
similarity of intention
with others
marks the fool from the
explorer

you can learn this at
any
poolhall, racetrack, bar
university or
jail.

people run from rain but
sit
in bathtubs full of
water.

it is fairly dismal to know that
millions of people are worried about
the hydrogen bomb
yet
they are already
dead.

yet they keep trying to make
women
money
sense.

and finally the Great Bartender will lean forward
white and pure and strong and mystic

to tell you that you've had
enough
just when you feel like
you're getting
started.

The Ants

I was down by the mill at last,
and I saw a rabbit go by
and a rotten log
and a rotten heart,
and I sat and smoked on a stump
and I watched the ants;
the ants are everywhere
picking up the dead,
their dead and the other dead,
cleaning up the earth,
and the sky was the same old
pale blue
like a weak water color,
and a couple of clouds,
fat and senseless;
and I took out the bottle
and the notebook
and I was a man a thousand years old,
and a thousand years back
or a thousand years ahead,
and I looked down into the oil of water
and the sun came back
painting blurs in my head,
showing me who was master
and how weak I was
and I put my hand flat on the dirt
palm up
and the ants came up
and touched
and passed around
so I guessed that I was not dead,
but no, there was one,
he came up and climbed
and I could feel the thin hair-legs
as he climbed

both of us brilliant in the sunlight,
and then down he went into the dirt,
and he ran ahead, but the next one ran
up my sleeve and then out,
and then stood there in my palm, blind,
looking up at me, and while he stood there
another came up and touched his feelers
and they talked about me,
and then came a third and a fourth
and I felt their excitement:
this palm in the dust could be theirs,
and I rose with a curse
and pinched and blew them off
like the idiots they were:
their time would come to share with the worm,
but this time this time was mine!
but no matter that I walked off into the pines
and frightened a squirrel,
they had said,
they'd had their say,
and I was done.

Suicide

he told me he had all the gas on
without flame
but when I got there
at 11:30 p.m. the gas was flaming and
he was drunk on the couch
with his ragged goatee:
"it got too much," he told me,
"I got to thinking
and it got too much."

which is good enough, we who think
or work with words, we who carve
can come up against this, especially
if we believe our early successes
and believe the game is won.

I think of Ernie tagging himself
when the time was ready
and I think of Frost
going on,
licking the boots of politicians,
telling the pretty lies
of an addled mind,
and I think,
well, Ernie's won
another round.

I pour the kid a drink, then
pour myself one. kid?
hell, he's 30. a lady's man
and a master of the English
language with a
peanut-shell soul.

and I? and I? nothing more.
we drink and he reels off
petty larcenies. later I leave,
both of us alive.

the next Sunday, I'm told,
my friend was in Frisco
in a green bow tie
reading his poems to a
society of misplaced ladies.

I'm told he
gassed them to
death.

3:30 A.M. Conversation

at 3:30 a.m. in the morning
a door opens
and feet come down the hall
moving a body,
and there is a knock
and you put down your beer
and answer.

god damn it, she says,
don't you ever sleep?

and she walks in
her hair in curlers
and herself in a silk robe
covered with rabbits and birds

and she has brought her own bottle
to which you splendidly add
2 glasses;
her husband, she says, is in Florida
and her sister sends her money and dresses,
and she has been looking for a job
for 32 days.

you tell her
you are a jockey's agent and a
writer of jazz and love songs,
and after a couple of drinks
she doesn't bother to cover
her legs
with the edge of the robe
that keeps falling away.

they are not bad legs at all,
in fact, very good legs,

and soon you are kissing a
head full of curlers,

and the rabbits are beginning
to wink, and Florida is a long way
away, and she says we are not strangers
really because she has seen me
in the hall.

and finally
there is very little
to say.

Cows in Art Class

good weather
is like
good women—
it doesn't always happen
and when it does
it doesn't
always last.
a man is
more stable:
if he's bad
there's more chance
he'll stay that way,
or if he's good
he might hang
on,
but a woman
is changed forever
by
children
age
diet
conversation
sex
the moon
the absence or
presence of the sun
or good times.
a woman must be nursed
into subsistence
by love
where a man can become
stronger
by being hated.

147

I am drinking tonight in Spangler's Bar
and I remember the cows
I once painted in Art class
and they looked good
they looked better than anything
in here. I am drinking in Spangler's Bar
wondering which to love and which
to hate, but the rules are gone:
I love and hate only
myself—
the others stand beyond me
like oranges dropped from the table
and rolling away; it's what I've got to
decide:

kill myself or
love myself?
which is the treason?
where's the information
coming from?

books . . . like broken glass:
I wdn't wipe my ass with 'em
yet, it's getting
darker, see?

(we drink here and speak to
each other and seem knowing.)

paint the cow with the biggest
tits
paint the cow with the biggest
rump.

the bartender slides me a beer
it runs down the bar
like an Olympic sprinter
and the pair of pliers that is my hand

stops it, lifts it,
golden, dull temptation,
I drink and
stand there
the weather bad for cows
but my brush is ready
to stroke up
the green grass straw eye
sadness takes me over
and I drink the beer straight down
order a shot
fast
to give me the guts and the love to
go
on.

Practice

I keep practicing death
and as the worms writhe
in agony of waiting
I might as well have another
drink, and I am thinking
I am *there*:
and I cross my legs
in the patio of
some Mexico City hotel
in 1997
and the birds come down
to pick out my eyes
and the birds fly away
and I no longer see
them.

is it shotguns of cancer
or sun-madness?

the rotting of the heart,
the gut, the lily.

now there's Hem. I always thought of Hem
as a tough old guy frying a steak
in some kitchen
under a bright light. what
happened, Ernie?

Hem was practicing too.
Everytime he watched a bull die
he got ready. when he lit a cigar
at four in the afternoon, he
got ready.

the bulls, the soldiers, the cities
the towns . . .

my sadness, my sadness
(let me have this drink)
could be strung across guitars
everywhere
and played for 10 minutes
with all the generals bowing
whores little girls again
maids kissing my photograph
on the plaza wall   haha
and old warriors
rubbing their blue stiff veins
and hoping for one more day
of bravery.

I practice for you, death:
your wig
that dress
your eyes
these teeth.

I too am an old man frying a steak
in a small kitchen.

when I run out of luck
I'll run out of whiskey
and when I run out of whiskey
the land will not be green,
and my love and my sadness . . .
who needs these?

I practice death pretty good:
send in the bull
send in the girl whose white flesh
maddens men on the boulevards,
send in Paris,

send in a car on the freeway
with 6 people going to a picnic,
send in the winner of the 8th,
send in Palm Beach and all the people
on the sand!
and I practice for you
too,
and the man sweeping the sidewalk
and the lady in bed with me
and the poems of Shakespeare
and the elephants
and the queers and the murderers,
I practice for everybody,
but for myself mostly.

pouring another drink now
at 9:30 in the morning,
the Racing Form on the couch,
the mailman walking toward me
with a loveletter from a lady who
doesn't want to die and a letter from the
government
telling me to give them money;
and I practice for the government too,
and I'm red, all red inside,
punctured with heart and intestine and lung,
I hope they don't arrest me,
I practice pretty good
and I've got a steak, a cigar
and a fifth of scotch,
I've read most of the classics
and I watch the birds fly this morning
and I can see most of them,
many of them that you can't see,
and I'm going to take a bath pretty soon,
put on some clean clothes
and drive South to the track.

it is not an unusual morning except that
it is one more,
and I want to thank you
for listening.

I Kneel

these legs need to run
but I kneel
before female flowers
catch the scent of
forgetfulness
and grab it
sure
and evenings
hours of evenings
grey-headed evenings
nod
and afterwards
fall asleep.

Freedom: The Unmolested Eagle of Myself

justification of blood and rock is
justification of you
waiting in the doorway

justification of gun and club and pincers is
justification of you
spreading a tablecloth

the tree's mathematics is the pounding dull leaves of
your eyes

my feet pushed into socks is an Arab crawling up to
kill

juice of christ in a pear is myself driving away
at 90 miles an hour

        and

the flak and the gruel and the words are riveted to the
walls
        they are

packaged like bombs to explode under my
enemies

and the evening comes down smiling and humming one
more dead tune

        and

it's hooray: look out: wait:
starve and be covered by dirt until
life is tall and silver
again.

Singing Is Fire

the birds are on fire
now
out there
and I walk across the room
and hold back the shade
and they are out there now
burning at
5:05 a.m.—darkness lifting like a
horse falling through sand. well,
I've got a blazer of whiskey left and
there are enough stretchers to carry the dead
but
not enough water to save the burning
birds: and *they* are telling me now:
        FLAME!   FLAME!
                        FLAME!
as old trains move through the
desert
as the whores sleep with the job
done
as the schoolboys dream of laborless
love
        the birds BURN and
        die before me—
        they
fly away done
leaving the grass for what's left of the
worms   what's left of the worms
        what's left of them
        for what's left of me:
old tin song with lunatic tears:

            which
is nothing new
except it's different now

feeling so bad
they used to call it the blues
but it's not so bad
whatever you call it
because at this time of light
say 5:36 a.m.
I still have a little whiskey left and
therefore a
chance.

and the sun wields mercy
but like a torch carried too high,
and the jets whip across its sight
and rockets leap like toads,
and the boys get out the maps
and pin-cushion the moon,
old green cheese,
no life there but too much on earth:
our unwashed India boys
crossing their legs, playing pipes,
starving with sucked-in bellies,
watching the snakes volute
like beautiful women in the hungry air;
the rockets leap,
the rockets leap like hares,
clearing clump and dog
replacing out-dated bullets;
the Chinese still carve
in jade, quietly stuffing rice
into their hunger, a hunger
a thousand years old,
their muddy rivers moving with fire
and song, barges, houseboats
pushed by the drifting poles
of waiting without wanting;
in Turkey they face the East
on their carpets
praying to a purple god
who smokes and laughs
and sticks his fingers in their eyes
blinding them, as gods will do;
but the rockets are ready: peace is no longer,
for some reason, precious;
madness drifts like lily pads
on a pond, circling senselessly;

the painters paint dipping
their reds and greens and yellows,
poets rhyme their loneliness,
musicians starve as always
and the novelists miss the mark,
but not the pelican, the gull;
pelicans dip and dive, rise,
shaking shocked half-dead
radioactive fish from their beaks;
indeed, indeed, the waters wash
the rocks with slime; and on Wall St.
the market staggers like a lost drunk
looking for his key; ah,
this will be a good one, by God:
it will take us back to the
snake, the limpet, or if we're lucky,
the catalysis to the
sabre-teeth, the winged monkey
scrabbling in the pit over bits
of helmet, instrument and glass;
a lightning crashes across
the window and in a million rooms
lovers lie entwined and lost
and sick as peace;
the sky still breaks red and orange for the
painters—and for the lovers,
flowers open as they have always
opened but covered with the thin dust
of rocket fuel and mushrooms,
poison mushrooms; it's a bad time,
a dog-sick time—curtain,
act III, standing room only,
SOLD OUT, SOLD OUT, SOLD OUT again,
by god, by somebody and something,
by rockets and generals and
leaders, by poets, doctors, comedians,
by manufacturers of soup
and biscuits, Janus-faced hucksters

of their own indexterity;
I can see now the coal-slick
contaminated fields, a snail or 2,
bile, obsidian, a fish or 3
in the shallows, an obloquy of our
source and our sight . . .
has this happened before? is history
a circle that catches itself by the tail,
a dream, a nightmare,
a general's dream, a president's dream,
a dictator's dream . . .
can't we awaken?
or are the forces of life greater than we?
can't we awaken? must we forever,
dear friends, die in our sleep?

On the Failure of a Poet

pinch-penny light, rifted, pitied light
like the drunken face of God in the sand,
smiling forgiveness . . . some old candle burning
in some old house
on the last night of earth,
house burning,
earth burning
in tears and poetry
scorching the filthy stars.

stalwart death, clean-up batter,
picking his nose and his victims,
old buddy, chewing stale bread,
always successful
as I listen to the crickets
while the master poets snore,
as I bring up the walls of China
in my poor brain
and walk them in wet dark
dropping lilies into ponds
calling to the dead
who have crawled away to hide;
while the master poets snore
I pay homage to bombs
the face of Baune turning to blood
with only the eyes holding still to the edge of sunset,
not wanting to go down . . .

now I cling evilly to these walls
and stand before a mirror
examining my content:
I represent rent, cheap labor
and nickle-coffee nights,
dancer in the splendid hock-shops
and rooms that close across the throat

as words fly from my small white hands
as the master poets snore . . .

are their birds more silken than mine?
perhaps, perhaps . . . it is so hard to deny!
what trick hikes their wings?
I tell you, no sparrow is more carved or
craving than mine . . . and yet
across my window
no voice answers, nothing responds;
I hear only the electric voices,
the shuffling of plates and lives,
on and on
these same simple dead sounds
enfolding me in their unchallenged weight,
while the master poets sing
and are praised,
and even fools love and are loved;
faith burns away:
I am a beggar hoisting lulled
sacked thoughts,
knowing I have the bolt to throw
but the catcher's out of sight.

The Beast

Beowulf may have killed Grendel and
Grendel's mother
but he
couldn't kill this
one:
it moves around with broken back and
eyes of spittle
has cancer
sweeps with a broom
smiles and kills
germs germans gladiolas

it sits in the bathtub
with a piece of soap and
reads the newspaper about the
Bomb and Vietnam and the freeways
and it smiles and then
gets out naked
doesn't use a towel
goes outside
and rapes young girls
kills them and
throws them aside like
steakbone

it walks into a bedroom and watches
lovers fuck
it stops the clock at
1:30 a.m.
it turns a man into a rock while he
reads a book

the beast
spoils candy
causes mournful songs to be

created
makes birds stop
flying

it even killed Beowulf
the brave Beowulf who
had killed Grendel and Grendel's
mother

look
even the whores at the bar
think about it
drink too much and
almost
forget business.

A Rat Rises

in some suburban cellar
a rat rises and tongues the leaky bottom of your life;
dreams of Cairo leave the body first,
such a November!—sweet pain tickling
like a fly, brushed off, it circles back
and settles again . . .
I will not lie: I hear the cackle of the grave
on nights that cannot be drunk away,
and it has rained all this same day
and buying my paper
I saw the drops falling
from the newsboy's hat
to his nose
and then falling from his nose . . .
but I doubt he ever considered
cutting his throat,
ending a quick love.
Ramsey, says a voice on the phone,
Ramsey, you sound so damned sad!
downstairs a child draws circles in the mud,
it has stopped raining.
circles, circles
weep less, wonder less.

I hear a voice singing.
I open a window.
a dog barks.
in Amsterdam a holy man trembles.

Pansies

pansies in a glass
this is sterile
sterile meaning
less trouble,
the arms of color
lifting
like cobras,
everything standing
around the glass
in the room.
I am thinking
of the
bee.

The Man with the Hot Nose

I am stuck with a snarl,
by God,
that would walk up the side
of a house;
I snarl, kissing maidens,
50-year-old whores
and torn-up mutuel
tickets;
all affected, I think,
as the motorcycle cop
writes out his ticket
and I think of myself
killing him,
laying him in the sunlight
badge upwards
for butterflies
and stares;
I snarl when I shit
or read the
stock market quotations;
I snarl when it rains,
I am almost depraved,
seldom laugh,
misunderstand flat tires
and various things
such as
human decay of mind and
body, spiders at
work,
all the dead troops of
forever,
toy crosses for sale
in stationery store
windows,
elephants for sale

or thirsty,
riot for useless
causes; stuck elevators,
constipation,
I understand nothing
except maybe
falling off a couch
drunk;
ariel ariel by God,
the clown's tin sides
thumping,
I bring the cigarette
close,
light it,
not setting my hair
on fire
(I guess this is
important);
I snarl a bit
in case there is Anybody
on the stairway,
on the roof,
on the mountain,
pissing from the tower of
Pisa (which must be
leaned back a bit
for ten million dollars)
and looking.

Hangover and Sick Leave

I know very little
and while I have eyes inside my head,
and feet to walk with, and
there are universities and
books full of men and
places like
Rome and Madrid—
I stay in bed
and watch the light rise in the curtains
and listen to the sounds
that I dislike, and
I fear the angry wife
the landlord
the psychiatrist
the police
the priest,
yet in bed here
the sun of myself working around my
bones
I am real enough
while
thinking of the factory workers with
sweating crotches
I know enough
of Los Angeles
in this room
so that there is nothing to
prove
and I raise the covers
to the ears of my empty head
and breathe in and out
in and out
within these walls
the beautiful cardboard day of
the mole.

Mercy, Wherever You Are, Come Running in to Me and Grab Me in Your Good Arms—

sterile faces squeezed out from squalid tubes of
bodies ream and blind me to any
compromise.
I would crawl down into the black volcanic gut of a
chicken and
hide hide hide.
listen, I know you think I am bitter and
maybe insane, well
that's all right
but find me a place:

a doorman at the casino
where I may separate the drunks from their
florins
or let the air out of the tires of the
mayor
until the years pass by and they
burn the world
until the difference in faces is
indifferent.
or now look
while I'm asking for things
I'd like to tell you
this:
I would like a piece of ass
I have always wanted a piece of ass
most of the
time.
I mean good
stuff   not like what
I've been
getting.
                              I want all
silk and garters and flesh and

snake wriggle and the
diamond earrings and the
accent, and the smell of
small cotton
animals.
I don't ask for a field of flowers in a
coal mine.
I don't ask you to put eyes in the bats in the
cave.
I don't ask you to dissolve the bombs like
snow.
I don't ask pet lions on the front lawn or a
free train ride to
St. Louis.
just a few things.
either that or I've got to sell the
piano.

It's Nothing to Laugh About

there's no color like the color of an orange,
and the mountains were a sad smokey purple like
old curtains in some cheap burlesque house;

and the small toad sat there
holding the dusty road like a tiny tank,
and staring,
staring like something really definite,
a greener living green than any green leaf;
and it puffed its sides and let them fall
and sometimes through the skin you could see
the dark water of another world;
and then it shot the blood through one eye—
you could see the guts contract
gripped by the glove of the skin—and
the red-thin stream of frogblood
a bright neat trick of centuries
hurled through bright valley air
upon golden nylon;

she screamed and he laughed, delighted with
the frog's great victory; she rubbed a quick
pink hanky against the desecrated nylon—
some womanly female in her had been splashed
and unveiled and defeated, and her dress hung
like some loose and second skin as the
indelicate horror writhed in her and claimed away
her fullness;
"you fool!" she spit over the stocking, "it's
nothing to laugh about!"

he looked at the toad in the fine rustbrown road
and imagined it smiled at him—
and then it turned half-sideways and hopped left
without haste

and popped again into the air
like some slow-motion nature film,
the leg-ends seeming to grip for notches in the air
and the head humped stiff
and brutalized away from life
like an old man reading a newspaper;
and then, with a backward over-the-shoulder look
it hopped into the grass of home;

"he's gone," he spoke sadly.
he looked to the rocks of the purple mountains
and sensed the frog moving toward them,
done with cities and roads;
he imagined the frog in a stream
his green skin happy against the blue-chill water;

he took her hand and they moved forward
together
over the unguarded road.

35 Seconds

failures. one after the
other. a whole duckpondfull
of failures. my
right arm hurts way
up into my shoulder.

it's like at the track.
you walk up to the bar
your eyes scared out of
your head and
you drink it down:
bar   legs   asses
walls   ceiling
program
horseturds

and you know you
only have 35 seconds left to live
and all the red mouths
want to kiss you,
all the dresses
want to lift and
show you leg,
it's like bugles
and symphonies
everywhere
like war
like war
like war

and the bartender leans
across and says
I hear they're going to
send in the 6

174

in the next
race.

and you say
fuck you,
and he is
a white dishtowel
in your grandmother's house
which is no longer
there.

and then he says
something.

and that's how
I hurt my
arm.

Regard Me

regard me in high level of terror
as the one who pulled down the shades
when the president stopped to shave,
enthralled by the way the Indian turned
through darkness and water and sand;
regard me as the one who laughed
when the cat caught fire in the radio
and the owl blew his stinking stack
grabbing mice and bulls and ornaments;
regard me as the one who picked the meat
from the bones and shot craps with God
as the poison coronets floated in the air;
regard me, even as dead, more alive than
many of the living,
and regard me, as I fumble with flat breasts,
regard me as nothing
so we may have peace
and forget.

With Vengeance Like a Tiger Crawls

to hell with metric—I have read the lore of the ages
and placed them back on their lifeless shelves:
we have written ourselves insensible
while outside . . .
to hell with poesy—I would rather sit
in cheap burlesque houses
and watch the sick Irish and Jewish clowns
spill their rank wit
into thimble minds.
ah, I know the clouds are quicker than we think
and that we fail at center,
spread outward
like so much ink
and quickly die;
so being a poltroon, I have read the classics,
I have argued in the marketplace,
I have been drunk with the immortals:
I have listened to these children cry
that language is too huge a bone for all of us:
even the finer wits have dulled their massive teeth.

all the waters are wasted
on Cadillacs and dahlias,
and I am wasted on Milton and matchsticks . . .
and, tonight, closer to madness than I have ever known,
I watch a small yellow bird
eat gravel at the bottom of his cage.
oh, let me lose my father's face!
. . . and find a forest all the axmen execrate,
let me be fuddled in the glade
numb with the growth of fancy;
let me find men and dogs and children,
let me find towers and lattice swaying
                                    in the sun
and a God of Life instead of Death.

when they deal their sticks against my brain
let me see dogs and goats and islands
and clasp my hands beneath their might
(to hell with your bright wit,
with vengeance like a tiger crawls)
and flying, flying
    reach Israel
    the waters
    a stone of blue
    all round in midnight

ah, I want too much!
bring on your voices, gallant but gall,
chill me with garlic and horns
and yawn me glibly through the
last candle of my hours: I will die
witless and poor.

Itch, Come and Gone

words   words like steel
like a copper bodice,
like flamingoes
their bloody straw legs
caught under rock;
words as ridiculous
as the equator
as pitiful and clumsy
as some mongrel dog
scratching
working away at an itch
in the skin;
then
there are other tools:
other ways
some shine and some sing
and there are some that spin
and some that kill,
but always,
back to the word:
it will describe your painting
your statue—

words
to end a fable
that no longer itches
anywhere

now ridiculous but not clumsy
pitiful
but not wrong.

This

I have refused the discipline
of Art and Government and
God and all that which
destroys my seeming
and lifting my beer now
frothy
in the golden afternoon
light
I have it:
plateaus of softness, wire
leaves, spirit of the sidewalks
walls that weep like old paintings
everything real, not bent,
and as a brown sparrow
drops across my window's sight
and the planes graze Africa again
in fire-lit nightmare
I have all I need on this tablecloth:
sunflower seeds, can opener
razor, 2 pencils, bent paper clip
memory of sparrow, angular sidewalk—
this under my fingers
myself myself myself.

2 Outside, As Bones Break
in My Kitchen

they get up on their garage roof
both of them 80 or 90 years old
standing on the slant
she wanting to fall really
all the way
but hacking at the old roofing
with a hoe

and he
more coward
on his knees praying for more days
gluing chunks of tar
his ear listening
for more green rain
more green rain
and he says
mama be careful

and she says nothing
and hacks a hole
where a tulip
never grew.

Saying Goodbye to Love

no more stalling,
the war torch is lit
and all over the neighborhood
men rattle in their irons,
flares kite the sky
somebody rushes past,
a confused cock crows
and I strike up
a cigarette.

it is difficult to decide
where the enemy is:

I go inside
to wife and hound
both fat and soft
as peaches
under the
sun.

I shave by candlefat and lightning,
I shave by their holy silence
in a shattered mirror.

I put on my hat
and hug them both
like two jellychildren
lost in smoke;
then outside I go,
searching the West
(dim and hilly
I'm told)
with bright
mean eyes.

You Smoke a Cigarette

You smoke a cigarette in fury and fall into
neutral slumber, to awaken to a dawn of
windows and grieving, without trumpets; and
somewhere, say, is a fish—all eye and movement—
wiggling in water; you could be that
fish, you could be there, held in water,
you could be the eye, cool and hung,
non-human; put on your shoes, put on
your pants, boy; not a chance, boy—
the fury of the absent air, the scorn of those alike
as dead violets; scream, scream, scream
like a trumpet, put on your shirt, your
tie, boy: grieve is a pretty word like
mandolin, and strange like artichoke; grieve is
a word and grieve is a way; open the door,
boy; go away.

Friendly Advice to a Lot of Young Men

Go to Tibet.
Ride a camel.
Read the bible.
Dye your shoes blue.
Grow a beard.
Circle the world in a paper canoe.
Subscribe to *The Saturday Evening Post*.
Chew on the left side of your mouth only.
Marry a woman with one leg and shave with a
        straight razor.
And carve your name in her arm.

Brush your teeth with gasoline.
Sleep all day and climb trees at night.
Be a monk and drink buckshot and beer.
Hold your head under water and play the violin.
Do a belly dance before pink candles.
Kill your dog.
Run for Mayor.
Live in a barrel.
Break your head with a hatchet.
Plant tulips in the rain.

But don't write poetry.

Everything

the dead do not need
aspirin or
sorrow,
I suppose.

but they might need
rain.

not shoes
but a place to
walk.

not cigarettes,
they tell us,
but a place to
burn.

or we're told:
space and a place to
fly
might be the
same.

the dead don't need
me.

nor do the
living.

but the dead might need
each
other.

in fact, the dead might need
everything we
need

and
we need so much,
if we only knew.
what it
was.

it is
probably
everything

and we will all
probably die
trying to get
it

or die

because we
don't get
it.

I hope
you will understand
when I am dead

I got
as much
as
possible.

fucker, you might at least send me a couple of your
books
I don't read anymore unless
I get them free
you write a good letter but then
a lot of them write good
letters
but when it comes to writing the poem
they dry up and die like a
wax museum.

and, baby, I see you've been around:
Evergreen Review, Poetry etc.
I cannot
make these golden outhouses of
culture and have long since
given up.

I will never have a house in the valley with
little stone men to water my
lawn.

as I get older
(and I am getting older)
I can look at a green gardenhouse
(not mine)
for hours or I can look at
these swinging elephant ears outside the
window
they are caught between the wind and me and
the sinking sun
and the sea is 20 miles west and
I have not seen the sea for maybe 3
years and

maybe it's not there anymore and maybe I'm
not here, anymore.

and the only time I begin to feel
is when I drink the yellow beer down so fast and so
long that the electric light bulb glows like the
sun and my woman looks like a highschool girl with
schoolbooks and
there is not a dent in the world and
Pound has shaved and
the bulldog smiles.

now,
for a cigarette. cancer and I
have an understanding like a
whore paid for. I haven't been to a
charity ward and been slugged to my knees for some
time
all the stale blood everywhere like
puke
and I keep thinking that there have been men who
died for something or
thought they did
and so
there's this sense of waste
just dying for yourself with
nobody around
not even a nurse
just
this
old man of 80
yelling at you down on the floor while you are
hemorrhaging,
yelling from his bed:
         "shut up! I want to SLEEP!"

well, he'll get his
sleep.

One Hundred and Ninety-Nine Pounds
of Clay Leaning Forward

the chain is on the door
the naked women shut out
the naked power on as I
bend over turbine-powered
sun-powered jets
knowing that I am not very good at
going on—
I'd rather watch a beetle crawl the sick
powdered dust of
earth—
while you are aware of my
cold handshake and
my cigar more alive than my
eyes, my
wit dimmer than
last Fall's sunlight.
but, Christ, friends—
the luger, the mortar, the patchwork
as I gape out at you from a
porkchop mouth—
take me as Caesar was taken
or
Joan of Arc
or
the man who fell off the fire escape drunk
or
the suicide at Bellevue
or Van Gogh confused with
ravens
and the atomic yellow.

I hold everything away from myself
so that you may become
real and shaking and stemmed
and ascending and blue and buttermilk

as the chorus girls kick out,
flags wave,
the eagle sinks into the sea,
as
our dirty time is just about
served and done.

I Write This Upon the Last Drink's Hammer

grief-tailed fish,
Sunday-eye in walking shorts
with staff,
motorcades in honor of the roots
of trees,
the rain like a young girl
walking toward me,
the houses waving like flags
filled with drunken hymns,
the bulls of Spain
the bulls of Spain
winning
unpracticed as leaves
as alone as shrimp upon a sea-bottom
or if this is wrong
as alone as what is there,
as my love
an old woman with rouged cheeks
skips rope again
as Hemingway's fingers live again
tough and terrible and good,
as Kid Gavilan once again flurries
like hyacinths into Spring,
I am sad I am sad I am sad
that the tongue and teeth will eat us
must choose so many good
like these fingers of lilies into the brain
sock out light
to those of us who sit in dark rooms alone
on Monday mornings
while presidents speak of honor and culture
and dedication;
or orange moon of moaning
that my voice speaks like slivers through a broken
face,

all this time I've seen through the bottoms of bottles
and black oil wells pumping their stinking arms
ramming home to the core of a rose
split into shares split into dividends
that tinkle less than the grunt of a frog,
I am hammered home not upon wisdom
but upon defamation:
old cars in junk yards,
old men playing checkers in the park,
women putting a price upon the curve of leg and breast,
men going to education like a bank account
or a high-priced whore to accompany them to a symphony,
one-third of the world starving while
I am indecent enough to worry about my own death
like some monkey engrossed with his flea,
I am sad because my manliness chokes me down
to the nakedness of revulsion
when there is so little time to understand,
I am sad because my drink is running low
and I must either visit people who drink
or go to storekeepers
with a poem they will never print,
strings of an avant-garde symphony
upon my radio,
somebody driving a knife through the everywhere cotton
but only meaning
that he protests dying,
and I have seen the dead
like figs upon a board
and my heart gone bad
breaking from the brain and reason
left with only
the season of
love
and
the question:
why?
that Wagner is dead say

is bad enough
to me
only
or that Van Gogh
does not see the strings and puddles
of this day,
this is not so good,
or the fact that
those I have known to touch
I am no longer able to touch;
I am a madman who sits in the front row
of burlesque shows and musical comedies
sucking up the light and song and dance
like a child
upon the straw of an icecream soda,
but I walk outside
and the heinous men
the steel men
who believe in the privacy of a wallet
and cement
and chosen occasions only
Christmas New Year's the 4th of July
to attempt to manifest a life
that has lain in a drawer like a single glove
that is brought out like a fist:
too much and too late.
I have seen men in North Carolina mountains
posing as priests when they had not even
become men yet
and I have seen men in odd places
like bars and jails
good men who posed nothing
because they knew that posing was false
that the blackbird the carnation the dollar bill in the palm
the poem for rested people with 30 dollar curtains plus
time for flat and meaningless puzzles,
they knew the poem the knife
the curving blueing cock of Summer

that all the love that hands could hold
would go would go
and that the needs for knicknacks and gestures
was done
o fire hold me in these rooms
o copper kettle boil,
the small dogs run the streets,
carpenters sneeze,
the barber's pole itches
to melt in the sun,
come o kind wind of black car
as I cross Normandy Avenue
in a sun gone blue
like ruptured filaments of a battered suitcase,
to see where you are to see where you have gone
I enter the store of a knowing Jew, my friend,
and argue for another bottle
for him
and
for me
for
   all
     of
       us.

Poem for Liz

the bumblebee
is less than a stack of
potato chips,
and growling and groaning
through barbs
searchlight shining into eyes,
I think of the good whore
who wouldn't even
take god damn easy money
and when you slipped it into her purse
she'd find it
and slap it back
like the worst of insults,
but she saved you from the law
and your own razor
only meant to shave with

to find her dead later
in a three-dollar-and-fifty-cent-a-week room,
stiff as anything can stiffen,
never having complained
starved and laughing
only wanting one more drink
and one less man
only wanting one small child
as any woman would
coming across the kitchen floor toward her,
everything done up in ribbons and sunshine,

and when the man next to the barstool
that stood next to mine
heard about Liz
he said,
"Too bad, god damn, she was a fine piece."

No wonder a whore is a whore.

Liz, I know, and although I'd like to see you
now
I'm glad
you're dead.

A Nice Place

It isn't easy running through the halls
lights out trying to find a door
with the jelly law
pounding behind you like the dead,
then #303 and in, chain on,
and now they rattle and roar,
then argue gently,
then plead,
but fortunately
the landlord would rather have his door
up than me down
in jail . . .

". . . he's drunk in there
with some woman. I've warned him,
I don't allow such things,
this is a nice place, this is . . ."

soon they go away;
you'd think I never paid the rent;
you'd think they'd allow a man to drink
and sit with a woman and watch the sun
come up.

I uncap the new bottle
from the bag and she sits in the corner
smoking and coughing
like an old Aunt from New Jersey.

Insomnia

have you ever been in a room
on top of 32 people sleeping
on the floors below,
only you are not sleeping,
you are listening to the engines
and horns that never stop,
you are thinking of minotaurs,
you are thinking of Segovia
who practices 5 hours a day
or the graves
that need no practice,
and your feet twist in the sheets
and you look down at a hand
that could easily belong to a man
of 80, and you
are on top of 32 people sleeping
and you know that most of them
will awaken
to yawn and eat and empty trash,
perhaps defecate,
but right now they are yours,
riding your minotaurs
breathing fiery hailstones of song,
or mushroom breathing:
skulls flat as coffins,
all lovers parted,
and you rise and light a cigarette,
evidently,
still alive.

the foreign hands and feet that tear my window shades,
the masses that shape before my face and ogle
and picture me relegated to their damned cage
         failed and locked
         quite finally in; . . .
the fires are preparing the burnt flowers of my hills,
the wall-eyed butcher spits
and flaunts his blade
backed by law, dullness and admiration—
how the girls rejoice in him: he has no doubts,
he has nothing
and it gives him strength
like a bell clanging against the defenseless air . . .

there is no church for me,
no sanctuary; no God, no love, no roses to rust;
towers are only skeletons of misfit reason,
and the sea waits
as the land waits,
amused and perfect;

carefully, I call voices on the phone,
measuring their sounds for humanity and laughter;
somewhere I am cut off, contact fails;
I return the receiver
and return also
to the hell of my undoing, to the looming
larks eating my wallpaper
and curving fat and fancy in the bridgework
of my tub,
and waiting against my will
against music and rest and color
against the god of my heart
where I can feel the undoing of my soul
spinning away like a thread
on a quickly revolving spool.

When the Berry Bush
Dies I'll Swim Down the Green
River with My Hair on Fire

the insistent resolution like
the rosebud or the anarchist
is eventually
wasted
like moths in towers
or bathing beauties in
New Jersey.

the buses sotted with people
take them through the streets of
evening where Christ
forgot to weep
as I move down move down
to dying
behind pulled windowshades
like a man who has been gassed or stoned
or insulted by the days.

there goes a rat stuck with love,
there goes a man in dirty underwear,
there go bowels like a steam roller,
there goes the left guard for Notre Dame in
1932, and like Whitman
I have these things:

I am a face behind a window
a toothache
an eater of parsley
a parallel man staring at ceilings of night
a heaver of gas
an expeller of poisons
smaller than God and not nearly as sure
a bleeder when cut

a lover when lucky
a man when born.

there's much more and much less.

at 6 o'clock they start coming in like the
sea or the evening paper, and like the leaves of the
berry bush outside they are a little sadder now,
inch by inch now it's speckled with brown and falling leaves,
day by day it gets worse like a wart haggled with a pin;
my shades are down as the scientists decide how
to get to Mars,
how to get out of
here. it is evening, it is time to eat a pie, it is time for
music.

Whitman lies there   like a sandcrab   like a frozen
turtle   and I get up and walk across
the room.

Face While Shaving

So what is a body but a man
caught inside
for a little while?
staring into a mirror,
recognizing the vegetable clerk
or a design on wallpaper;
it is not vanity that seeks reflection
but dumb ape wonder;
but still the reflection . . .
movement of arm and muscle, shell-head,
a face staring down through the
stale dimension of dreams
as a Mississippi coed powders her nose
and paints a lavender kiss;
the phone rings like a plea
and the razor breaks through the snow,
the dead roses, the dead moths,
sunset after sunset,
steam and Christ and darkness,
one tiny inch of light.

9 Rings

the simple misery of survival
the tyranny of ancient rules
and new deaths,
the coming of the beetle-winged
enemy
chanting, cursing
bits of blood and grit;
I slam my fingers
in the window
as the phone rings.
I count 9 rings
and then it stops;
some voice it was
to test my reality
when I have no reality,
when I am water
walking around bone
in a green room.

I would burn the swans
in their lake,
I would send messengers
to the mountaintop
to razz the clouds.

she was getting to be a
dull lay
anyway.

hey man! somebody yells down to me through my broken
window,
> ya wanna go down to the taco stand?

hell, no!
> I scream from down on the floor.

why not? he asks.

> I yell back, who are you?

none of us knows who we are, he states, I just thot maybe you
wanted to go down to the taco
stand.

> please go away.

no, I'm comin' in.

> listen, friend, I've got a foot of salami
> here and the first fink that walks in,
> he's gonna get it in the side of his
> head!

don't mess with me, he answers, my mother played halfback for
St. Purdy High for half-a-year before somebody found her
squatting over one of the
urinals.

oh yeah, well, I've got bugs in my hair, mice and fish in
my pockets and Charles Atlas is in my bathroom
shining my mirror.

with that, he leaves.

I get up, brush the beercans off my chest
and yell at Atlas to get the humping hell out of there,
I've got
business.

Thank God for Alleys

hummingbird make yr mark he said and then something about
an arab and a son of a bitch and I hit him in the mouth and
we fought in the snow for ten minutes spotting it with red
blossoms—breathing is a blade—and I kept thinking of astronauts
up there circling the earth like a rowboat around a pond
all out of trouble and in trouble, and we finally stopped
or somebody or something stopped us and we went into Harry's
for a drink and the place was empty and Harry kept looking
at us as if he hated us and pretty soon we began to hate him
his money, his hate, his hate of us without as much money
or as much hate, and my friend threw his glass against Harry's
mirror and then he *did* hate us, and we ran out down the alley
and the dogs barked, and the only essence that was left
was remembering
the time
the last time I was asleep
and the earth obeyed
everything.

The Millionaire

look at him
a withered man

sure
he's been thru a
bit

he was under the covers and the house shook with the
bombardment

he smiled out at
us

I hope I never get that
old

a slice of wall shook free and fell across his
bed

they say he was a tough boy
they say he was worth millions

sunlight poked thru a hole in the
wall
sunlight and smoke and a
treebranch

I had almost finished ripping out the plumbing
looking for something valuable
but there was nothing
left

somebody had been there
earlier

"let's go"

when we got to the top of the hill
a shell landed right in the middle of where we'd
left

it was boards flying and him down in there
and then a fire came—
fast
red
perfect

we went into the woods and Harry threw a rock at a
squirrel and
missed.

Dow Jones: Down

how can we endure?
how can we talk about roses
or Verlaine?
this is a hungry band
that likes to work and count
and knows the special laws,
that likes to sit in parks
thinking of nothing valuable.

this is where the stricken bagpipes blow
upon the chalky cliffs
where faces go mad as sunburned violets
where brooms and ropes and torches fail,
squeezing shadows . . .
where walls come down en masse.

tomorrow the bankers set the time
to close the gates against our flood
and prevaricate the waters;
bang, bang the time,
remember now
        the flowers are opening in the wind
        and it doesn't matter finally
        except as a twitch in the back of the head
when back in our broad land
dead again
we walk among the dead.

As I Lay Dying

The time comes to go deeper
into self and the time comes
when it is more innocent
or easier to die
like bombers over
Santa Monica,
and I remember
laying there in the sand,
myself 20 years old,
reading Faulkner
because the name sounded good
and being vaguely excited
by something
that was not myself
and closing the book
and getting
sick of the sea
and the sky
blue blue blue
spots of white,
all dizzy in the trap,
wanting out
but knowing
I was nailed
like the sand-fleas
I slapped at,
and Mr. Faulkner
laying on his side
immortal and burning
with my toes
and everything tilting
and not quite
true.

A Minor Impulse to Complain

well
it's interesting what does go on,
and what doesn't go on
that should,
and the world's quite a sight
spun through spiders and webs
that catch us half asleep
and do us in
before we're even old enough
to know we're through

if it isn't a whore it's a wife,
and if it isn't a wife
it's a jam over taxes
or bread or liquor,
or somebody's slipping it into her
while you're down at the shop
sweating your nuggets to keep her in silk.

or you're on horses or pot
or crossword puzzles,
or you're on vitamins or Beethoven.

but you oughta see
what goes on on a 75 foot yacht:
it would make you give up
liberty and little magazines
and Tolstoy
to see what beautiful young ladies can do
to somebody else.

and he doesn't even care,
and he'll tell you
pouring a short shot,
that bitch'd outscrew a rabbit,

and unless you've got money
by the time you got it figured out
you're either so old you're senseless
or you're so old you're dead.

and there she stands by the rail
looking good
golden sun and real gold,
the fish going by in the largest swimming pool
in the world, and she even smiles at you
as you go below to get more bottles and boots
and to scrape the barnacles from the master;
but, ah, you pig!—he told me all you did,
as men will do—which is another way of saying
you and I ain't living well,
or enough.

Buffalo Bill

whenever the landlord and landlady get
beer-drunk
she comes down here and knocks on my door
and I go down and drink beer with them.
they sing old-time songs and
he keeps drinking until
he falls over backwards in his chair.
then I get up
tilt the chair up
and then he's back at the table again
grabbing at a
beercan.

the conversation always gets around to
Buffalo Bill. they think Buffalo Bill is
very funny. so I always ask,
what's new with Buffalo Bill?

oh, he's in again. they locked him
up. they came and got him.

why?

same thing. only this time it was a
woman from the Jehovah's Witness. she
rang his bell and was standing there
talking to him and he showed her his
thing, you know.

she came down and told me about it
and I asked her, "why did you bother that
man? why did you ring his bell? he wasn't
doing anything to you!" but no, she had to
go and tell the authorities.

he phoned me from the jail, "well, I did it
again!" "why do you keep doing that?" I
asked him. "I dunno," he said, "I dunno
what makes me do that!" "you shouldn't do
that," I told him. "I know I shouldn't do
that," he told me.

how many times has he done
that?

Oh, god, I dunno, 8 or 10 times. he's
always doin' it. he's got a good lawyer, tho,
he's got a damn good
lawyer.

who'd you rent his place to?

oh, we don't rent his place, we always keep his
place for him. we like him. did I tell you about
the night he was drunk and out on the lawn
naked and an airplane went overhead and he
pointed to the lights, all you could see
was the taillights and stuff and he pointed to
the lights and yelled, "I AM GOD,
I PUT THOSE LIGHTS IN THE SKY!"

no, you didn't tell me about
that.

have a beer first and I'll
tell you about it.

I had a beer
first.

Experience

there is a lady down the hall who paints
butterflies and insects
and there are little statues in the room,
she works with clay
and I went in there
and sat on the couch and had something to drink,
then I noticed
one of the statues had his back turned to us,
he stood there brooding, poor bastard,
and I asked the lady
what's wrong with him?
and she said, I messed him up,
in the front, sort of.
I see, I said, and finished my drink,
you haven't had too much experience with men.
she laughed and brought me another drink.
we talked about Klee,
the death of cummings,
Art, survival and so forth.
you ought to know more about men,
I told her.
I know, she said. do you like me?
of course, I told her.
she brought me another drink.
we talked about Ezra Pound.
Van Gogh.
all those things.
she sat down next to me.
I remember she had a small white mustache.
she told me I had a good life-flow
and was manly.
I told her she had nice legs.
we talked about Mahler.
I don't remember leaving.

I saw her a week later
and she asked me in.
I fixed him, she said.
who? I asked.
my man in the corner, she told me.

good, I said.
want to see? she asked
sure, I said.
she walked to the corner and turned
him around.

he was fixed, all right

my god, it was ME!

then I began to laugh and she laughed
and the work of Art stood there,
a very beautiful thing.

I Am Visited by an Editor and a Poet

I had just won $115 from the headshakers and
was naked upon my bed
listening to an opera by one of the Italians
and had just gotten rid of a very loose lady
when there was a knock upon the wood,
and since the cops had just raided a month or so ago,
I screamed out rather on edge—
who the hell is it? what you want, man?
I'm your publisher! somebody screamed back,
and I hollered, I don't have a publisher,
try the place next door, and he screamed back,
you're Charles Bukowski, aren't you? and I got up and
peeked through the iron grill to make sure it wasn't a cop,
and I placed a robe upon my nakedness,
kicked a beercan out of the way and bade them enter,
an editor and a poet.
only one would drink a beer (the editor)
so I drank two for the poet and one for myself
and they sat there sweating and watching me
and I sat there trying to explain
that I wasn't really a poet in the ordinary sense,
I told them about the stockyards and the slaughterhouse
and the racetracks and the conditions of some of our jails,
and the editor suddenly pulled five magazines out of a portfolio
and tossed them in between the beercans
and we talked about *Flowers of Evil*, Rimbaud, Villon,
and what some of the modern poets looked like:
J. B. May and Wolf the Hedley are very immaculate, clean
    fingernails, etc.;
I apologized for the beercans, my beard, and everything on the
    floor
and pretty soon everybody was yawning
and the editor suddenly stood up and I said,
are you leaving?
and then the editor and the poet were walking out the door,

217

and then I thought well hell they might not have liked
what they saw
but I'm not selling beercans and Italian opera and
torn stockings under the bed and dirty fingernails,
I'm selling rhyme and life and line,
and I walked over and cracked a new can of beer
and I looked at the five magazines with my name on the cover
and wondered what it meant,
wondered if we are writing poetry or all huddling in
one big tent
        clasping assholes.

The Mexican Girls

whichever way you turn
there is gauze and the needle,
the back turned to light,
scars like valleys
scars like pits of terror,
and the peach falls to
the dirt.

the hospitals are the same
most grey like old balloons,
these sidewalks
they are so sweet
leading to the beds
where they shit upon
themselves,
my hands again locked,
sick twigs of limbs,
hurricane here:
minds going out
like lighthouse lamps

hell hell
so much sick

and they come up to change
the sheets, 2 mexican girls
without even a sneeze
or pause
and one of them points at
me: "I'll take this one
and you take that one
and we'll make them well
and then we'll
all
shack-up together!"

and they laugh

and the clean sheet comes
down bringing in the cool
air, and I hear them
walk away laughing
and the trees are filled
with fruit, the sun
brings gophers peeking
from their holes; stones
are these which stick in
shoes, that pounce upon
the hollow head
that cannot bleed or
kiss; I touch the sheets,
I touch the sheets . . .

The New Place

I type at a window that faces the street
on ground level and
if I fall out
the worst that can happen is a dirty shirt
under a tiny banana tree.

as I type people go by
mostly women
and I sit in my shorts
(sometimes without top)
and going by they
can't be sure I am not entirely
naked. so
I get these faces
which pretend they don't see
anything
but I think they do:
they see me as I
sweat over the poem like beating a
hog to death
as the sun begins to fail over
Sunset Blvd.
over the motel sign
where tired people from Arkansas and Iowa
pay too much to sleep while
dreaming of movie stars.
there is a religionist next door
and he plays his radio loud
and it seems to have
very good volume
so I am getting the
message.
and there's a white cat
chewed-up and neurotic
who calls 2 or 3 times a day

eats and leaves
but just looking at him
lifts the soul a little
like something on strings.
and the same young man from the girlie
magazine phones and we talk
and I get the idea
that we each hang up
mildly thinking each other
somewhat the fool.

now the woman calls me to dinner.
it's good to have food.
when you've starved
food always remains a
miracle.
the rent is a little higher here
but so far I've been able to
pay it
and that's a miracle too
like still maybe being sane
while thinking of guns and sidewalks
and old ladies in libraries.
there are still
small things to do
like rip this sheet from the typer
go in and eat
stay alive this way.
there are lots of curtains waving here
and now the woman has walked in
she's rocking back and forth
in the rocker behind me
a bit angry
the food is getting cold and
I've got to go
(she doesn't care that
I've got to finish this thing).
it's just a poor little neighborhood

no place for Art,
whatever that is, and
I hear sprinklers
there's a shopping basket
a boy on roller skates.
I quit   I quit

for the miracle of food and
maybe nobody ever angry
again, this place and
all the other places.

Conversation in a Cheap Room

I keep putting the empties out back but
the kids smash them against the
wall almost as fast as I can drink them, and
old Mr. Sturgeon died and
they carried him down the stair and
I was in
my underwear; the rats ran after
him leaping with beautiful tails like the
tails of young whores half-drunk on
wine; I kept watching the
signal change outside and
my shoes sitting in the closet and
pretty soon people started coming
in, talking about death and
I watched a billboard advertising beer, and
we turned out all the lights and
it was dark and
somebody lit a cigarette and
we all watched the
flame; it warmed the
room, it put a glow on the walls and
there was a flaring concert of
liquid voices saying the
room is still here, the
drawers are
still here; Mrs. McDonald will
want her rent.

that's all they
said.

soon somebody went out for another bottle and
we were thinking of
something else.

I don't remember what, but
the
signal kept changing.

225

I don't remember what, but
the
signal kept changing.

225

I Was Born to Hustle Roses Down
the Avenues of the Dead

1

rivergut girlriver damn drowned
people going in and out of books and
doors and graves people dressed in pink
getting haircuts and tired and dogs and
Vivaldi

2

you missed a cat argument the grey was
tired mad flipping tail and he monkied
with the black one who didn't want to
be bothered and then the black one
chased the grey one pawed it once the
grey one said *yow*
ran away stopped scratched its ear
flicked at a straw popped in air and
ran off defeated and planning as a
white one (another one) ran along the
other side of the fence chasing a
grasshopper as somebody shot Mr
Kennedy.

3

the best way to explain the meaning
of concourse is to forget all about
it or any meaning at all
is
just something that grows or does not
grow lives a while and dies a long time
life is weak, the rope around a man's
neck is stronger than the man because

it does not suffer   it also does not
listen to Brahms but Brahms can get
to be a bore and even insufferable when
you are locked in a cage with
sticks almost forever.
I remember my old
man raged because I did not sweat
when I mowed his lawn twice over
while the lucky guys played football
or jacked-off in the garage, he threw a
2 by 4 at the back of one of my legs
the left one, I have a bloodvessel that
juts out an inch there now and I
picked up the log and threw it into
his beautiful roses and limped around
and finished the lawn not sweating
and 25 years later I buried him. it
cost me a grand: he was stronger
than I was.

4

I see the river now I see
the river now   grassfish
limping through milkblue
she is taking off her stockings
she is beginning to cry.
my car needs 2 new
front tires.

227

Winter Comes to a Lot of
Places in August

Winter comes in a lot of places in August,
like the railroad yards
when we come over the bridge,
hundreds of us,
workers, like cattle,
like Hannibal victorious over the Mountain;
Winter comes in Rome, Winter comes in Paris
and Miami
and we come
over the silver bridge,
carrying our olive lunch pails
with the good fat wives' coffee
and 2 bologna sandwiches
and oh, just a *tid-bit* found *somewhere*
to warm our gross man-bones
and prove to us that love
is not clipped out like a coupon;
. . . here we come,
hundreds of us,
blank-faced and rough
(we *can* take it, god damn it!)
over our silver bridge,
smoking our cheap cigars in the grapefruit air;
here we come,
bulls stamping in cheap cotton,
bad boys all;
ah hell, we'd rather play the ponies
or chance a sunburn at the shore,
but we're men, *god damn it,* men,
can't you see?
men,
coming over our bridge,
taking our Rome and our coffee,
bitter, brave and
numb.

Bring Down the Beams

folding away my tools with the dead parts of
my soul
I go to night school, study Art;
my teacher is a homosexual who teaches us to
make shadows with
a 2b pencil (there are five laws of light, and it
has only been
known for the last 400 years
that shadows have a core);
there are color wheels,
there are scales
and there are many deep and futile rules
that must never be broken;

all about me sit half-talents, and suddenly—
I know
that there is nothing more incomplete than a
half-talent;
a man should either be a genius
or nothing at all;

I would like to tell that homosexual
(though I never will)
that people who dabble in the Arts
are misfits in a misshapen society;
the superior man of today is the man
of limited feeling
whose education consists of
ready-made actions and reactions to
ready-made situations;

but he is more interested in men than ideas,
and if I told him that a society which takes
its haircuts from characters in comic strips
needs more than heavenly guidance,

he would say
with sweeping and powerful irrelevance
that I was a bitter man;

so we sit and piddle with charcoal
and talk about Picasso
and make collages; we are getting ready
to do nothing unusual
and I alone am angry
as I think about the sun clanging against the earth
and all the bodies moving
but ours;

I would bring down the world's stockpile of drowned
and mutilated days!
I would bring down the beams of sick warehouses
I have counted
with each year's life!
I want trumpets and crowing,
I want a red-palmed Beethoven rising from the grave,
I want the whir and tang of a simple living orange
in a simple living tree;

I want you to draw like Mondrian, he says;
but I don't want to draw
like Mondrian,
I want to draw like a sparrow eaten by a cat.

Reunion

the love of the bone
where the earth chewed it down, that's
what lasts,
and I remember sitting on the grass
with the negro boy,
we were sketching housetops and
he said,
you're leaving some out,
you're cheating,
and I walked across the street
to the bar
and
then he came in—
you are due back in class
at 2, he told me,
then he left.

class doesn't matter, I thought,
nothing matters that we're told,
and if I am a fly I'll never know
what a lion really is.

I sat there until 4:30
and when I came out,
there he was.

Mr. Hutchins liked my
sketch, he told me.

that was over 20 years
ago.

I think
I saw him the other night.

he was a cop in the city jail
and he pushed me into
a cell.

I'm told
he doesn't paint
any
more.

Fragile!

I tried all night to sleep
but I couldn't sleep
and I began drinking
around 5:30
and reading about Delius
and Stravinsky,
and soon I heard them getting up
all over the building,
putting on coffee,
flushing toilets,
and then the phone rang
and she said,
"Sam, you haven't been in jail?"
"not lately,"
I told her,
and then she asked where the hell
I had been and all that,
and finally I got rid of her
and pulled up the shades
and put my clothes on,
and I went down to the coffeeshop
and they were all sitting there
with bacon and eggs.
I had a coffee and went on in.

I emptied the baskets and
ashtrays, put toilet paper
in the women's john
and then scattered the compound
to sweep. the old man came in
and eyed me riding the broom.
"you look like hell," he said, and
"did you
put paper in the ladies' room?"
I spit into the compound and

nodded. "that package to
McGerney's," he said. "12 pints
of floor wax . . ."
"yeah?" I asked.
"he says 7 of them pints
were broken. did you pack them right?"
"yeah."
"did you put FRAGILE labels
on them."
"yeah."
"if you run out of FRAGILE
labels, let me know."
"O.K."
". . . and be more careful
from now on."
he went into the office and
I swept on toward the back.
a few minutes later
I heard him laughing with
the secretaries.

I unlocked the back door, brought in
the empty trashcans, sat down and
    smoked
a cigarette. I began to get sleepy
at last.

one of the secretaries came back
rotating her can,
pounding her spikes
on the cement floor.

she handed me a stack of orders
to pick and pack, and this look, this
    smile
on her face saying—

I don't have to do much work,
but you do.

then she walked away wobbling,
wobbling meat.

I put some water in the tape machine
and stood there
waiting
waiting for 5:30.

I Am with the Roots of Flowers

Here without question is the bird-torn design,
drunk here in this cellar
amongst the flabby washing machines
and last year's rusty newspapers;
the ages like stone
whirl above my head
as spiders spin sick webs;
I can leech here for years
undetected
sleeping against the belly of a boiler
like some growthless
hot yet dead
foetus;
I lift my bottle like a coronet
and sing songs and fables
to wash away
the fantastic darkness
of my breathing;
oh, coronet, coronet:
sing me no bitterness
for I have tasted stone,
sing me no child's pouting and hate
for I am too old for night;
I am with the roots
of flowers
entwined, entombed
sending up my passionate blossoms
as a flight of rockets
and argument;
wine churls my throat,
above me
feet walk upon my brain,
monkies fall from the sky
clutching photographs
of the planets,

but I seek only music
and the leisure
of my pain; oh, damned coronet:
you are running dry!
. . . I fall beneath the spiders,
the girders move like threads,
and feet come down the stairs,
feet come down the stairs, I think,
belonging to the golden men
who push the buttons
of our burning universe.

Monday Beach, Cold Day

bluewhite birdlight
nothing but the motor of sand
noticing bits of life:
I and fleas and chips of wood,
wind sounds, sounds of paper
caught with its life flapping,
deserted dogs
as content as rock,
facing rump to sea
furred against sun and sensibility,
snouting against dead crabs
and last night's bottles . . .
everything dirty, really,
really dirty,
like back at the hotel,
the white jackets and 15^c tips,
the old girls skipping rope
not like young neighborhood girls
but for room, bottle and trinket,
and the hotel sits behind you
like grammar school and old wars
and you simply roll upon your stomach,
skin against warm dirty sand
and a dog comes up with his ice-nose
against the bottoms of your feet
and you howl angry laughter
through hangover and forty-year old kisses,
through guilty sun and tired wave,
through cheap memories that can never be
transformed by either literature or love,
and the dog pulls back
looking upon this stick of a white man
with red coal eyes
through filtered smoke,
and he makes for the shore, the sea,

238

and I get up and chase after him,
another hound, I am,
and he looks over a round shoulder,
frightened, demolished,
as our feet cut patterns of life,
dog-life, man-life,
lazy indolent life, gull-life
and running, and the sharks
out beyond the rocks
thrashing for our silly blood.

The High-Rise of the New World

it is an orange
animal
with
hand grenades
fire power
big teeth and
a horn of smoke

a colored man
with cigar
yanks at
gears and the damn thing never gets
tired

my neighbor
. . . an old man in blue
bathing trunks
. . . an old man
a fetid white obscene
thing—
the old man
lifts apart some purple flowers
and peeks through the fence at the
orange animal

and like a horror movie
I see the orange animal open its
mouth—
it belches it has teeth fastened onto a giraffe's
neck—
and it reached over the fence and it gets the
old man in his blue
bathing trunks

neatly
it gets him
from behind the fence of purple flowers
and his whiteness is like
garbage in the air
and then
he's dumped into a
shock of lumber

and then the orange animal
backs off
spins
turns
runs off into the Hollywood Hills
the palm trees the
boulevards as

the colored man
sucks red steam
from his
cigar

I'll be glad when it's all
over
the noise is
terrible and I'm afraid to go and
buy a
paper.

The Gypsies Near Del Mar

they live down by the sea . . . these men
and you see them going to the gray public bath
like colonels on parade;
they have trailers and dogs and wives and children
in that importance; they crawl upon the rocks
as turtles do and dream sun-dreams
turtle-dreams
that do not hurt;
—or you see them singly . . . standing with their poles
the sea climbing their ankles and ignored like some
useless oil
and their long lines search and wait beyond the breakers,
a vein from life to life and calm brisk death.

I have never seen their fish, or their gods
or the color of their eyes—though I imagine
the palest shade of pink,
like small-sweet pickled onions, and their bellies
like the bellies of jellyfish hiding in flowers
beneath the rock.

they are there all year, I'm told . . . these same men
with their rusty lives. when it rains the sand gets wet,
not as bad as mud, and they never die: you see
their fires at night as you drive back from the track,
nothing moving except the flame a little and the sea
changing shape, and you can see the threads of smoke
easing into the sky;
and as their camp goes by, leaving you vacant
you stare again into a world of red tail lights
and turn on the radio
and through the glass like the hand of some
forgotten god
you watch
a gull dip over your car
and then rise and fly out toward the sea.

6 A.M.

naked
unarmored
before the open window
sitting at the table
drinking tomato juice
the publicly unpardonable part
of my body
below the table
I watch
a man in an orange robe
and bedroom slippers
shit his dog upon the lawn
both of them
tempered by sparrows.

we are losers; even at high noon
or late evening
none of us dresses well
in this neighborhood
none of us studies the grace of high
finance
successfully enough
to shake
ugly things away
(like needing the rent or
drinking 59 cent wine).

yet now
the wind comes through the window
cool,
as pure as a cobra;
it is a sensible time
undivided
either by
explanation

deepeyed cats
life insurance or
Danish kings.

I finish the
tomato
juice and
go to
bed.

A Trick to Dull Our Bleeding

practically speaking
the great words of great men
are not so great.

nor do great nations nor great beauties
leave anything but the residue
of reputation to be slowly
gnawed away.

nor do great wars seem so great,
nor great poems
nor first-hand legends.

even the sad deaths
are not now so sad,
and failure was nothing but a
trick
to keep us going,

and fame and love
a trick to dull our bleeding.

and as fire becomes ash and steel
becomes rust, we become
wise
and then
not so wise.

and we sit in chairs
reading old maps,
wars done, loves done, lives done,

and a child plays before us like a monkey

and we tap our pipe and yawn,
close our eyes and sleep.

pretty words
like pretty ladies,
wrinkle up and die.

Rose, Rose

rose, rose
bark for me

all these centuries in the sun
you have heard men sing
to break like the stems that held you

you have sat in the hair of young girls
like roses themselves, feeling like roses,
and you know, you know what happened

I gave roses to a lady once and she put them
on her dresser and hugged them and smelled them
and now the lady is gone and the roses are gone
but the dresser is there, I see the dresser
and on the boulevards I see you again

alive again! yes!
and, I am still
alive.

rose, rose
bark for me

walking last night
feeling my flesh fat about my girth
old dreams faint as fireflies
I came upon a flower
and like a giant god gone mad
yanked off its head
and then put the petals in my pocket
feeling and tearing
soft insides, ha so!—
like defiling a virgin.

she hugged you, she loved you
and she died, and

in my room, hand out of pocket,
the first night's drink, and
along the edge of the glass,
the same same scarlet
virgin and thorn, my hand
my hand my hand; bark, rose
teeth of centuries blooming
in the sun, vast god damned
god pulling these poems out
of my head.

Spain Sits Like a Hidden Flower
in My Coffeepot

it is like tanks come through Hungary and
I am looking for matchsticks to
build a soul

it is the hunger of the intestine
and feeling sorry for a
radio dropped and broken last Tuesday night

Gertrude knows what is left of me
but she can hardly boil an egg and
she can't boil me
or put me together like
matchsticks
but some day I must send you
some of her poems or
her old shoe once worn by a
duchess

there isn't anybody on the street now
the street is empty and
Spain sits like a hidden flower
in my coffeepot as
the audience applauds the bones of
Vivaldi

and I could go on
tossing phrases like
burning candles
but I leave that to the
acrobats

a loaf of bread
dog bark
babycry

the matchless failure of
bright things

her leaning forward
over a cup of tea
telling me—
you are a kind man
you are a very kind
man

*

the eyes believing dynasties of softness
the hands touching my neck
the cars going by

the snails sleeping with pictures of Christ

I phrase the ending like hatchets
or a bush burned down
and kiss a staring
greenblue
eye

greenblue eye
like faded drapes the light burned through

and my god
another woman another night
going on

the rats are thimbles in cats' paws when it
rains in Miami
and the fence falls down

the world is on its back
legs lifted
and I enter again

into the
sweat and stink and torture—
a very kind man
gentle as a knife

the brilliant hush of parrots

Gertrude lives in a place by the freeway
and I live here—
the mice   the garbage   the lack of air
the gallantry

and
outside of here:
young girls skipping rope
strong enough to hang the men
now nowhere
about

me?:
        I dreamed I drank an Arrow shirt
        and stole a broken
        pail.

Thermometer

As my skin wrinkles in warning like
paint on a burning wall
fruitflies with sterile
orange-grey
eyes
stare at me
while I dream of lavender ladies as impossible
and beautiful as
immortality

as my skin wrinkles in warning
I read *The New York Times*
while spiders wrestle with ants in shaded roots
of grass
and whores lift their hands to heaven for
love
while the white mice
huddle in controversy over a
piece of cheese

as my skin wrinkles in warning
I think of Carthage and Rome and
Berlin
I think of young girls crossing their
nylon legs at bus stops

as my skin wrinkles in warning like
paint on a burning wall
I get up from my chair to drink water
on a pleasant afternoon
and I wonder about water
I wonder about me,
a warm thermometer kind of wonderment
that rises like a butterfly
in a distilled pale yellow afternoon

and then I walk back out
and sit on my chair
and don't think anymore—
as to the strain of broken ladders and old war
movies—
I let everything
burn.

Eaten by Butterflies

maybe I'll win the Irish Sweepstakes
maybe I'll go nuts
maybe
maybe unemployment insurance or
a rich lesbian at the top of a hill

maybe re-incarnation as a frog . . .
or $70,000 found floating in a plastic sack
in the bathtub

I need help
I am a fat man being eaten by
green trees
butterflies and
you

turn turn
light the lamp
my teeth ache the teeth of my soul ache
I can't sleep I
pray for the dead streetcars
the white mice
engines on fire
blood on a green gown in an operating room in
San Francisco
and I am caught
ow ow
wild: my body being there filled with nothing but
me
me caught halfway between suicide and
old age
hustling in factories next to the
young boys
keeping pace
burning my blood like gasoline and

making the foreman
grin

my poems are only scratchings
on the floor of a
cage.

Destroying Beauty

a rose
red sunlight;
I take it apart
in the garage
like a puzzle:
the petals are as greasy
as old bacon
and fall
like the maidens of the world
backs to floor
and I look up
at the old calendar
hung from a nail
and touch
my wrinkled face
and smile
because
the secret
is beyond me.

CHARLES BUKOWSKI is one of America's best-known contemporary writers of poetry and prose, and, many would claim, its most influential and imitated poet. He was born in Andernach, Germany, to an American soldier father and a German mother in 1920, and brought to the United States at the age of three. He was raised in Los Angeles and lived there for fifty years. He published his first story in 1944 when he was twenty-four and began writing poetry at the age of thirty-five. He died in San Pedro, California, on March 9, 1994, at the age of seventy-three, shortly after completing his last novel, *Pulp* (1994).

During his lifetime he published more than forty-five books of poetry and prose, including the novels *Post Office* (1971), *Factotum* (1975), *Women* (1978), *Ham on Rye* (1982), and *Hollywood* (1989). Among his most recent books are the posthumous editions of *What Matters Most Is How Well You Walk Through the Fire* (1999), *Open All Night: New Poems* (2000), *Beerspit Night and Cursing: The Correspondence of Charles Bukowski and Sheri Martinelli 1960–1967* (2001), and *The Night Torn Mad with Footsteps: New Poems* (2001).

All of his books have now been published in translation in over a dozen languages and his worldwide popularity remains undiminished. In the years to come, Ecco will publish additional volumes of previously uncollected poetry and letters.